Design for impact

Laurence King Publishing

Contents

Preface: The king of safety cards

One individual has played a part in the making of this book greater than any one of us working on it could ever have imagined. He is Carl Reese, probably the world's most avid collector of safety cards. Carl is also a significant producer of safety cards, through his company Cabin Safety. He has been extremely helpful, lending us some of his finest and rarest cards, as well as imparting his extraordinary knowledge of aviation history.

But where does the idea of collecting such an odd artefact as the safety card come from? Carl Reese explains:

Some people are collectors and other people aren't. And then there are people who just can't stop. They have to collect everything. My father is like that. He collected everything – stamps, coins, badges, junk. Well, mostly junk. He has a two-storey barn house completely filled with junk. And outside the house, scrap wood, wires and more useless stuff. There is no way you can change him. He is 71 years old. I inherited a part of that, but I only collect safety cards.

I was interested in planes and flying from the very beginning. I grew up just off the runway, close to Philadelphia Airport, and my Mom used to say that the first word to come out of my mouth, before I could say "Mom" or "Dad", was "airplane". On Sundays after church, when I was around eight or nine years old, my parents would take me to the airport, and they would just drop me off, giving me an hour there before picking me up again. Gradually they would extend the time to two hours, three hours, and finally it was like, "Give us a call when you're done". Of course, this was in the mid-1960s, long before airport security, so when the crews met a kid who was an airplane enthusiast, they would be more than happy to take him out to the aircraft and show him the cabins. Also, all the airlines were making money back then, so there was lots of publicity material, brochures and other stuff. I would exit the airport with my arms literally loaded with crap like timetables, postcards. Basically, you name it – I got it! It came to the point when my

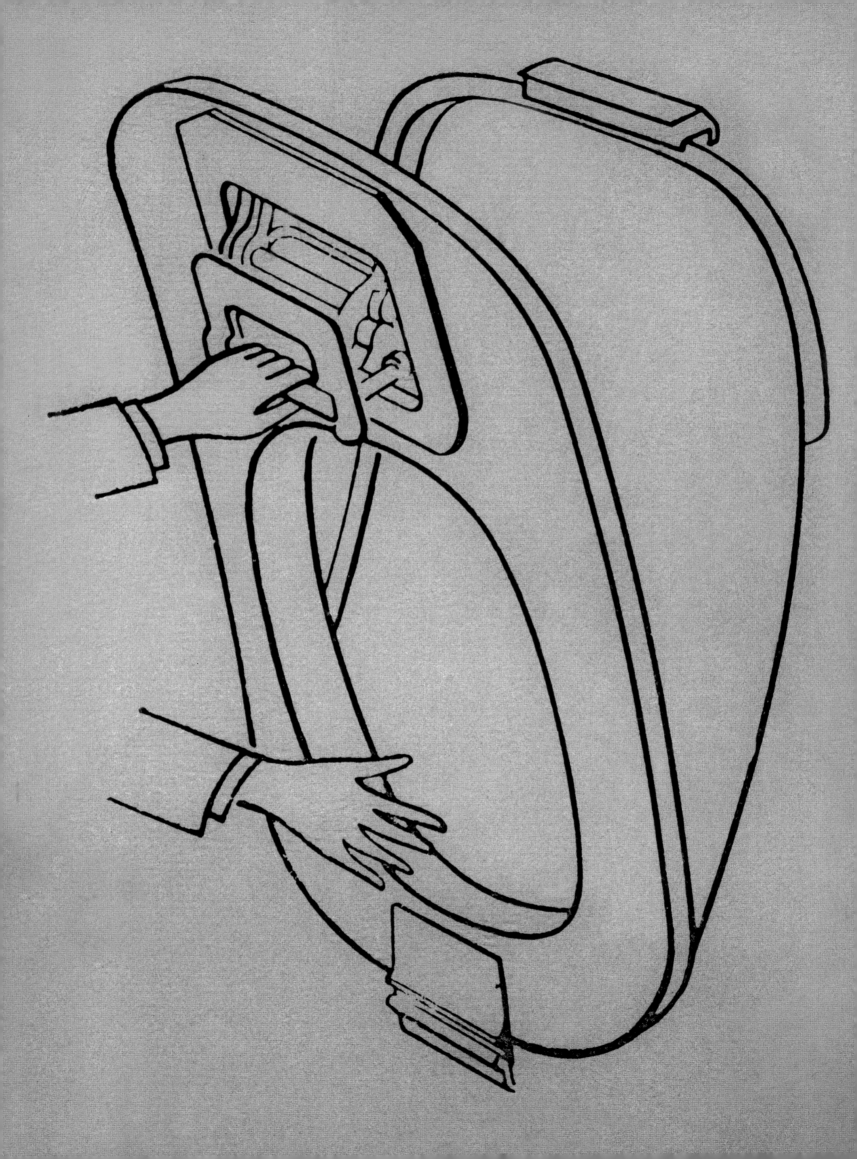

ماسك اكسیژن

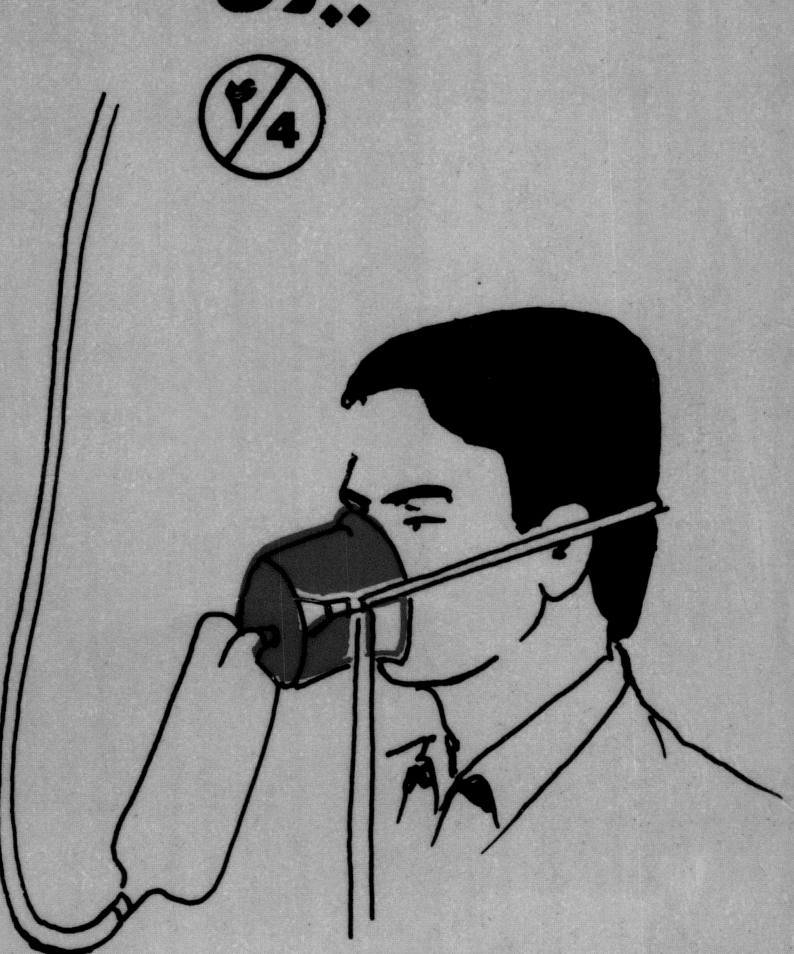

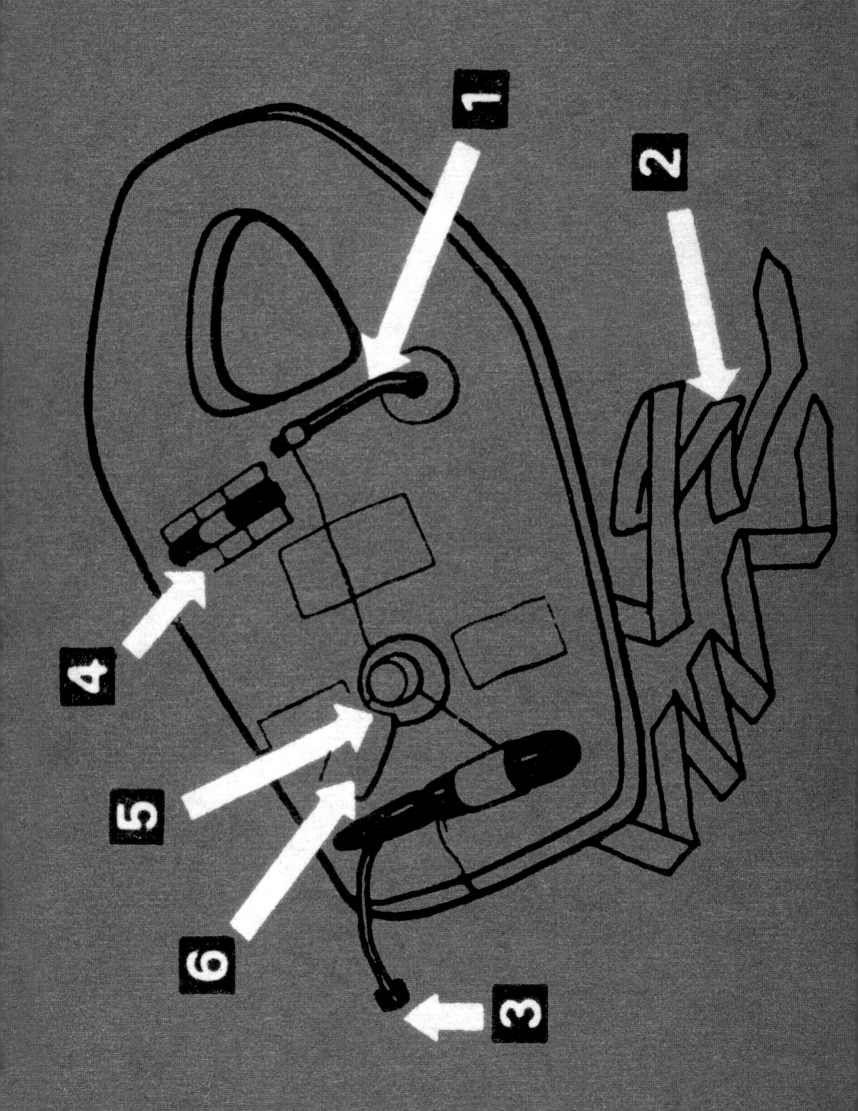

mother actually told me, "You have to decide on what you want to keep, because I can't get into your room anymore." The room was filled with stuff. So, I decided to keep the safety cards, since they were something unique: first of all, they were hard to find – you had to get on the airplane to get them. They weren't anything you could just pick up from the ticket counter. Secondly, they said something technical about the airplane, so I looked upon them as little pieces of equipment. That is basically how I got started – a couple of cards here, a couple of cards there, and the next thing I knew I had my dresser filled with nothing but safety cards. And then I started to ask friends of the family, who were travelling on business, to bring me safety cards, and so the collection grew.

And at this point, I decided that I wanted to work for an airline some day. I wanted to be a flight attendant. I never really wanted to be a pilot, mostly because I wore glasses and pilots weren't allowed to wear them in those days. I was very realistic. I always knew that I would work on board a plane. I graduated from high school early and got a job on an airline as a cabin attendant in 1971, when I was 17, just before I turned 18. Technically, you had to be 18 to work, but they were desperate for people for the Christmas season.

Designing safety cards kind of took off from the collecting. In the early 1970s, I worked for a company in Philadelphia called Downtown Airlines. It was a small commuter airline that didn't have any safety cards. They were rare on domestic flights. I approached the boss and asked if I could design some, and he replied "Yes, if they're not going to cost me anything!", and basically they didn't. In about 1980, my company, Cabin Safety, got going when I approached some of the local airlines and made proposals to design safety cards for them. And, from then on, it was word of mouth. People from other airlines saw my cards, called me, and things started to roll. Of course, in the beginning, there wasn't enough income from Cabin Safety for me to quit flying, so it was difficult. I flew internationally throughout my career, so I would come in from a trip, completely exhausted, and have to go right to work on the safety cards. Then, in 1991, Pan Am went out of business and I stopped flying. So I decided to devote all my time to Cabin Safety, and the company really took off.

I have no artistic education at all, but I have always drawn and sketched. Obviously, I sketched airplanes often when I was a kid. I also studied mechanical drawing in school, so I was always interested in clean work, straight lines, and everything had to be very precise. I guess that comes from my German background. My design abilities have developed over the years – when I look at my early cards today, they are so primitive that it is frightening! Now, my cards are much more precise and clean than they were in the beginning. I'm not usually inspired by the old cards in my collection. They might be pretty, but they are often very crude, and they wouldn't work as well as modern cards.

At the time of writing, Carl Reese holds a collection of no less than 70,000 safety cards from different periods and airlines.

Pre-war safety cards

The concept of flying in a machine was unnerving for most people 70 years ago. Nevertheless, there was no shortage of adventurous passengers for the early flights of the 1920s and 1930s. These daredevils usually paid a handsome price for their trip, with no guarantee of a safe arrival. Safety regulations in air travel were almost non-existent. The earliest safety cards typically handled flights over water, such as those crossing the English Channel, as these were the only flights for which safety regulations were drawn up. It is not hard to imagine the mind-boggling fear passengers must have felt when glancing at these early cards. They were strictly text-based, and would remain so for quite a while. They rarely showed the position of emergency exits, and told passengers to follow the orders of the crew in case of an emergency. There is, unfortunately, no record of when safety cards were first introduced, or whose idea it was to compile the safety information in a leaflet to be given to each traveller.

You are unlikely ever to need to wear one, but we always tell people what to do with a life-belt—because all our air liners crossing the sea carry them.

Put on the belt as you would a waistcoat so that the brass lever 'B' comes near or over your right hip, then hook the brass buckles in front of you.

To inflate the belt hold the air bottle, which you can feel inside the belt, in the left hand and press the lever 'B' upwards with the right hand. If the cylinder does not work, unscrew the valve 'A' on the left side of the belt, and blow the belt up with the mouth. Then screw the valve down tightly. You must not inflate the belt until after you have left the cabin. Emergency exits are provided in all the roofs of the cabins and are clearly marked. In the event of trouble these must be opened by the steward—not by the passengers

---

SOME OF THE OFFICES OF IMPERIAL AIRWAYS

LONDON
Airway Terminus, S.W.1 Telephone: Victoria 2211 (Day and Night)

PARIS
Airway Terminus, Rue des Italiens. Telephone: Taitbout 6050/1/2/3 (Day & Night)

BRUSSELS
19 Rue St. Michel. Telephone: Brussels 17.64.62

COLOGNE
Dom Hotel. Telephone: Rhineland 222774

BASLE
Birsfelden Aerodrome. Telephone: Basle 43880

ZURICH
Dubendorf Aerodrome. Telephone: Zurich 934201

LOCAL AGENT

Printed in Great Britain by Spottiswoode, Ballantyne & Co. Ltd., and published by Imperial Airways Limited IA/T/215 50m 2/34 *Stuarts*

Page 13. Pre-war safety card from Imperial Airways. This is probably one of the very first safety cards. It was printed in the early 1930s.

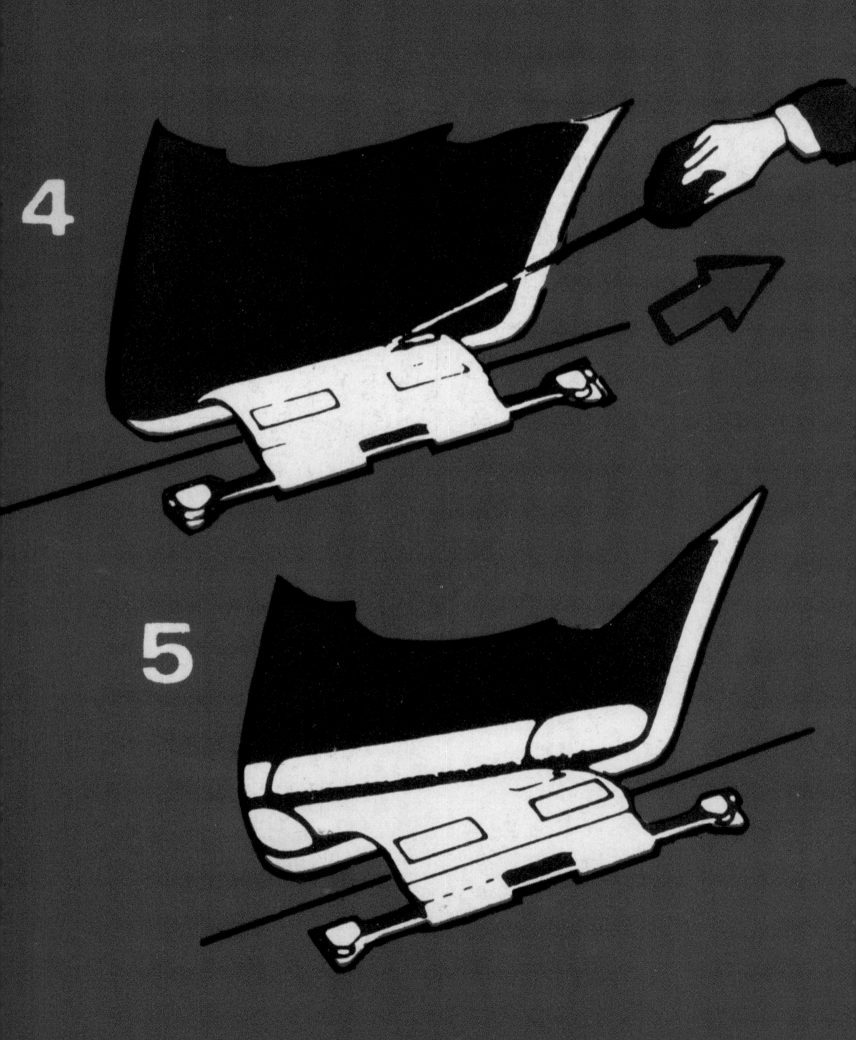

Post-war safety cards

The second world war brought the world many horrors, but it also brought about a tremendous leap forward in aviation engineering. Passenger aircrafts from the late 1940s onward had greater speed, reliability, comfort and safety than ever before. Air travel was still costly, but it was no longer deemed an adventure. Suddenly planes were reliable as well as fast. The capacity of the airplanes was still limited, however, and despite luxurious styling, comfort was not all it could be – passengers continued to endure the noise of the engines. Since the idea of flying was still quite terrifying for many travellers, one of the aims of safety cards from this time was to allay such fear. Slogans such as "life vests are fashionable and quite handsomely tailored", "no wet feet for you" and "don't take off any other clothes. You'll want to look your best when you land," were often accompanied by comic illustrations, making these cards amusing as well as attractive.

Richtlinien für Ihre
Sicherheit bei einer

Wasserlandung

Die Schlauchboote sind übrigens mit „allem Komfort" ausgestattet. So gibt es ausreichende Verpflegungs- und Trinkwasservorräte, eine Ausrüstung für „Erste Hilfe" und vor allem einen starken Sender, der in kürzester Zeit Hilfe herbeiholen kann. Und keine Sorge um den Platz im Boot - es gibt genügend Schlauchboote an Bord, um alle Passagiere und auch die Besatzung aufzunehmen.

So - und jetzt genießen Sie Ihren Flug in sicherer Höhe über den Wellen, und erfreuen Sie sich des soeben erworbenen Wissens, das Ihnen auch für den äußerst unwahrscheinlichen Fall einer Wasserlandung Schutz und Sicherheit gewährleistet.

LUFTHANSA

Wbg. 32 a / 456 / D-REL

Printed in Germany

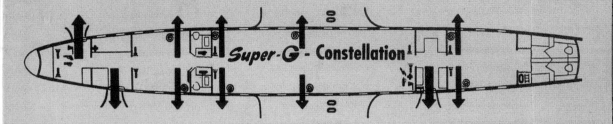

Super-G - Constellation

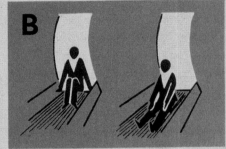

Benutzen der Rutsche

Wenn die Rutsche ausgebracht ist und von 2 Mann am Boden gehalten wird, springen Sie hinein und rutschen Sie hinunter (A). Ältere Personen nehmen vor dem Rutschen Sitzstellung ein (B). **Wichtig:** Nicht festhalten und nicht die Beine anziehen!

Using the chute

After the chute has been placed in position and is held on the ground by two people, enter the chute and slide to the ground (A). Elderly persons should slide down in a sitting position (B). **Important:** Do not hold on to the chute or raise or draw up your legs.

Utilisation du plan incliné

Quand celui-ci est sorti et solidement maintenu à terre par deux hommes, montez dessus et laissez-vous glisser jusqu'en bas (A). Les personnes âgées devront s'asseoir sur le plan incliné avant de commencer à descendre (B). **Recommandation importante:** Ne pas se cramponner et ne pas raidir les jambes.

Forma de usar el deslizadero

Una vez colocado el deslizadero hacia el exterior y mantenido junto al suelo por dos hombres, dé un salto y ubíquese en el mismo, deslizándose hacia el suelo (A). Tratándose de personas de alguna edad, conviene que se sienten, antes de deslizarse (B). **Importante:** !No aferrarse ni encoger las piernas!

Como servir-se do deslizador

Colocando o deslizador, que é seguro por dois homens no chão, entre nêle e deixe-se escorregar (A). Pessoas idosas, antes de deslizarem, devem ficar em posição de sentadas (B). **Importante:** Não se segure, e não encolha as pernas!

Sorties de secours

Si vous devez sortir par l'une des fenêtres de secours se trouvant au-dessus des ailes, fenêtre que vous ouvrira un membre de l'équipage, il faut passer d'abord une jambe, ensuite la tête, puis le reste du corps et enfin l'autre jambe.

Benutzung der Notausgänge

Müssen Sie das Flugzeug durch ein als Notausgang gekennzeichnetes Tragflächenfenster verlassen (das von einem Besatzungsmitglied geöffnet wurde), dann ist folgende Reihenfolge wichtig: ein Bein, Kopf, Oberkörper, anderes Bein.

Using the emergency exits

Should the need arise to leave the aircraft through one of the emergency exit wing windows (which has been opened by a crew member), we suggest the following sequence: first one leg, then the head, upper part of the body, and then the other leg.

Forma de usar las salidas de emergencia

En el caso que debiera abandonar el avión a través de una ventana del plano sustentador, caracterizada como salida de emergencia (que fuera abierta por un miembro de la tripulación), debe Vd. sacar primero una pierna, luego la cabeza, el torso y finalmente la otra pierna.

Como servir-se das saídas de emergência

Caso V. S. tenha que abandonar a aeronave através de uma janela (assinalada como saída de emergência) junto às asas e prèviamente aberta por um tripulante, observe atentamente a seguinte ordem: uma perna, a cabeça, o tronco e a outra perna.

LUFTHANSA

Anlegen der Schwimmweste

Stülpen Sie die Schwimmweste so über den Kopf, daß die kleine Lampe nach vorn und das breite Band nach hinten kommen (1). Befestigen Sie die Ringe an den vorderen Haken (2), und ziehen Sie an beiden Enden den Gurt stramm (3). Die Weste bläst sich selbsttätig auf, wenn Sie ruckartig an den beiden Knöpfen ziehen (4). Warten Sie aber damit, bis Sie das Flugzeug verlassen haben! Die Weste kann auch mit dem Mundschlauch aufgeblasen werden (5).
Jede Weste ist mit einer Signallampe ausgerüstet, die sofort aufleuchtet, wenn Sie die beiden Zäpfchen herausziehen und die Batterie ins Wasser fallen lassen.

Ablegen der Schwimmweste

Zum Ablegen der Weste erst die Luft herauslassen, dann auf die Schnallen drücken, den Gürtel lockern und die Haken lösen.

Donning the life jacket

(1) Pull the life jacket over your head in such a way that the signal lamp will be in front and the broad belt will be in the back. (2) Attach the rings to the front hooks, (3) pull the belt tight at both ends. (4) The life jacket is inflated by pulling the two buttons with a jerk. Please, refrain from doing so before having left the aircraft. (5) The life jacket may also be inflated by use of mouth tube.
Every life jacket is equipped with a signal lamp, which lights up immediately, if you pull the two levers and drop the battery into the water.

Removing the life jacket

In order to remove the life jacket, first deflate it and then press the buckles, and loosen the belt and the hooks.

Pour enfiler le gilet de sauvetage

Passez le gilet par-dessus votre tête de façon que la petite ampoule électrique vienne en avant et la bande large en arrière (1). Accrochez les anneaux au crochet de devant (2) et serrez énergiquement la ceinture par ses deux extrémités (3). Le gilet se gonfle automatiquement quand vous tirez d'un coup sec sur les deux boutons (4). Mais surtout, attendez d'être sorti de l'avion pour le faire! On peut aussi gonfler le gilet en soufflant dans l'embouchure (5). Le gilet comporte une ampoule électrique signalisatrice qui s'allume quand vous sortez les deux petits tenons et laissez tomber la pile dans l'eau.

Pour enlever le gilet de sauvetage

D'abord le dégonfler, ensuite appuyer sur les boucleteaux, dénouer la ceinture et libérer les crochets.

Forma de colocarse el chaleco salvavidas

Colóquese el chaleco salvavidas, pasándolo por la cabeza, de manera que la lamparita quede hacia adelante y la cinta ancha hacia atras (1). Fijar los anillos en los ganchos delanteros (2) y ajustar el cinturón en ambos extremos (3). El chaleco se infla automáticamente al tirar enérgicamente de los dos botones (4) — esperar no obstante hasta que haya Vd. abandonado el avión! El chaleco puede también inflarse mediante el tubo bucal (5).
Cada chaleco está provisto de una lámpara de señales, que se ilumina de inmediato al sacar Vd. los dos tapones y dejar caer al agua la batería.

Como sacarse el chaleco salvavidas

Para sacarse el chaleco, primero desinflarlo, luego presionar las presillas, aflojar el chaleco, desabrocharlo.

Como colocar o colête salva-vidas

Enfie a cabeça pela abertura do colête, de maneira que a pequena lâmpada fique na frente e a faixa larga atrás (1). Prenda as argolas nos ganchos da frente (2) e aperte o cinto, esticando-o pelas duas pontas (3).
O colête insufla-se por si mesmo desde que V.S. dê um puxão nos dois botões (4). Espere, porém, até depois de ter abandonado a aeronave! O colête pode ser insuflado também mediante o bocal de borracha (5).
Todo colête é provido de uma lâmpada que se acende tão logo V. S. tenha puxado os dois pinos, deixando a bateria cair n'água.

Como tirar o colête salva-vidas

Para tirar o colête, esvazie-o primeiro do ar; em seguida, aperte as fivelas, afrouxe o cinto e solte os ganchos.

Ausgang mit Notrutsche
Exit with Evacuation Chute
Sortie par le plan incliné
Salida con deslizador de emergencia
Saída com o deslizador

Notausstieg
Emergency Exit
Sortie de secours
Salida de emergencia
Saída por cima

Stablampe
Flashlight
Torche électrique
Linterna de emergencia
Lanterna de bôlso

Notbeil
Emergency Axe
Hache de secours
Hacha de emergencia
Machadinha

Feuerlöscher
Fire Extinguisher
Extincteur
Extinguidor de incendio
Extintor de incêndio

Notleiter
Emergency Ladder
Échelle de secours
Escalerilla de emergencia
Escada de emergência

Schlauchboot
Life-Raft
Canot pneumatique
Bote neumático
Bote de borracha

Sanitätskasten
First-Aid Kit
Boîte à pharmacie
Botiquín
Caixa de primeiros socorros

Notseil
Emergency Rope
Corde de secours
Soga de emergencia
Corda de emergência

Sende- und Empfangsgerät
Transmitter/Receiver
Émetteur-récepteur
Aparato emisor y receptor
Aparelho emissor e receptor

Leuchtpistole mit Munition
Very Pistol with Ammunition
Pistolet à fusées éclairantes avec son approvisionnement
Pistola para señales con munición
Pistola de foguetes e munição

Made in Germany (West)
Wbg.-Nr. 322 003 832/560/BTL

safety procedures

MESURES DE SECURITE

QANTAS EMPIRE AIRWAYS LTD.

AIR FRANCE — VISCOUNT 701

CONSIGNES DE SÉCURITÉ
SAFETY INSTRUCTIONS
CONSIGNAS DE SEGURIDAD

LE GILET DE SAUVETAGE • THE LIFE JACKET • EL CHALECO SALVAVIDAS

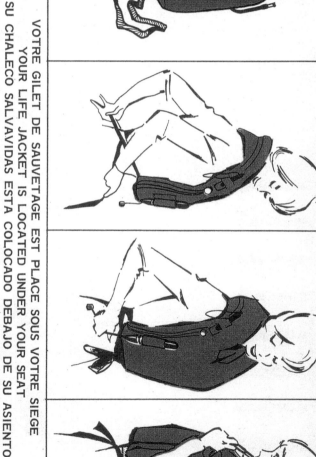
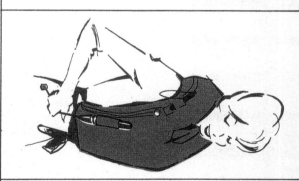

1 2 3 4

VOTRE GILET DE SAUVETAGE EST PLACE SOUS VOTRE SIEGE
YOUR LIFE JACKET IS LOCATED UNDER YOUR SEAT
SU CHALECO SALVAVIDAS ESTA COLOCADO DEBAJO DE SU ASIENTO

LE GILET DE SAUVETAGE
YOUR LIFE JACKET
EL CHALECO SALVAVIDAS

Enfilez-le par la tête
nouez les sangles devant

Pour le gonflage, tirez sur
la petite boule rouge

Utilisez éventuellement le
tube de gonflage bucal

*

Pull it over your head
tie in front the two tapes

To inflate, pull sharply the
little red ball

If necessary, use mouth-
piece to inflate

Les gilets des enfants doivent
être gonflés AVANT de quitter l'avion.

Pase la cabeza por la
abertura

Para la inflada, tirar la
bolita roja

Eventualmente, utilizar el
tubo de inflado a boca

Children must inflate their
jacket's BEFORE leaving the
aircraft.

Los chalecos de los niños
deben ser inflados ANTES de
salir del avión.

anude las cinchas por de-
lante.

AIR FRANCE VISCOUNT 701

CONSIGNES DE SÉCURITÉ

SAFETY INSTRUCTIONS

CONSIGNAS DE SEGURIDAD

EVACUATION ET MATERIEL DE SECOURS • EMERGENCY EXITS AND SAFETY EQUIPMENT • EVACUÁCION Y EQUIPO DE SOCORRO

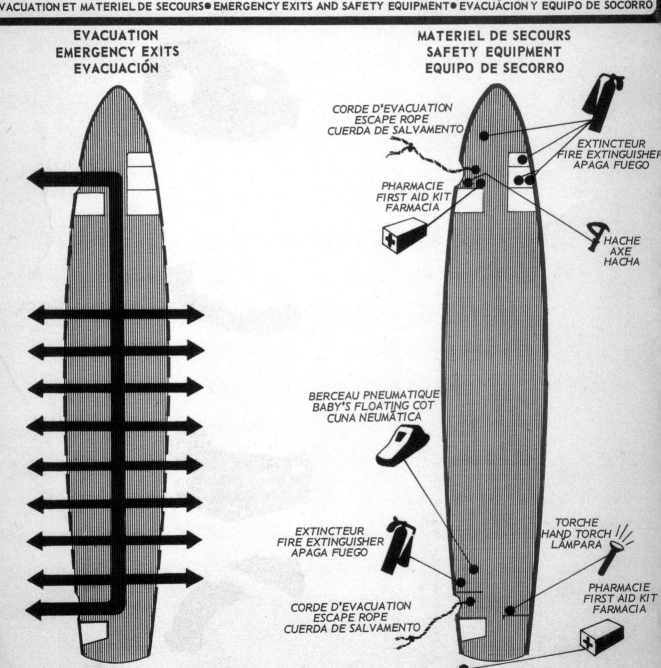

EVACUATION
EMERGENCY EXITS
EVACUACIÓN

MATERIEL DE SECOURS
SAFETY EQUIPMENT
EQUIPO DE SECORRO

CORDE D'EVACUATION
ESCAPE ROPE
CUERDA DE SALVAMENTO

EXTINCTEUR
FIRE EXTINGUISHER
APAGA FUEGO

PHARMACIE
FIRST AID KIT
FARMACIA

HACHE
AXE
HACHA

BERCEAU PNEUMATIQUE
BABY'S FLOATING COT
CUNA NEUMÁTICA

EXTINCTEUR
FIRE EXTINGUISHER
APAGA FUEGO

TORCHE
HAND TORCH
LÁMPARA

CORDE D'EVACUATION
ESCAPE ROPE
CUERDA DE SALVAMENTO

PHARMACIE
FIRST AID KIT
FARMACIA

You are now flying on an Eastern Air Lines Golden Falcon Super-G, one of the world's most dependable airliners. Your pilots and crew are skilled and experienced. There is little likelihood that we will ever be forced to land on water, but it is good practice to be acquainted with the facilities Eastern has provided for your safety.

WHERE TO FIND YOUR LIFE VEST

Life vests are located in a holder under each seat in the cabin.

Your life vest is easily inflated and will keep you afloat and right side up, come what may. Do not remove the life vest from the sealed bag unless actually necessary, as it has been inspected and sealed in the package to insure its proper functioning.

HOW TO PUT ON YOUR LIFE VEST

Ⓐ Put on life vest over head.
Ⓑ Fasten buckles; pull tight around waist.
Ⓒ Jerk gas release knobs AFTER YOU LEAVE PLANE.
Ⓓ If later the vest becomes too soft, it may be inflated orally.

WHAT TO DO IN CASE OF AN EMERGENCY LANDING ON WATER

Remain calm and follow instructions of crew.

Get your life vest and put it on.

Put the back of your seat in the upright position and fasten your seat belt.

Sit in emergency landing position—lean forward, lower head between legs, clasp hands under legs, tense muscles.

When plane is completely stopped, unfasten seat belt. Inflate your life vest *only after you have left the plane.* Follow crew's instructions for leaving aircraft and boarding life raft.

This aircraft maintains regular, frequent radio contact with Eastern's Flight Control Dept. In the event of an emergency, search and rescue facilities will immediately be put into action.

LIFE RAFTS—This aircraft carries enough 20-man life rafts to accommodate all passengers and crew members in the event of an emergency landing on water. In all instances, your flight crew, who have been thoroughly trained and drilled in emergency procedures, will launch and inflate the life rafts. Life rafts are equipped with all necessary supplies—emergency rations, first aid kit, etc.

LOCATION OF LIFE RAFTS AND EMERGENCY EXITS

Circles show number of life rafts at each location. Arrows show emergency exits.

Emergency Exits—In addition to the main cabin door, this aircraft is fitted with emergency exits. These exits are located at certain windows on both sides of the cabin and are clearly labeled. To open exits:

1. Remove the plate covering the exit handle.
2. Pull red exit handle inward and down.
3. Grip handle at bottom of exit and pull into cabin.

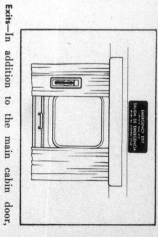

Usted está volando ahora en El Halcón de Oro Super-G de la Eastern Air Lines, uno de los aviones más confiables del mundo. Sus pilotos y tripulación son expertos. Hay muy poca probabilidad de que nos veamos forzados a amarizar, pero es prudente que usted conozca las facilidades que la Eastern ha provisto para su seguridad.

DONDE LOCALIZAR SU CHALECO SALVAVIDAS

Los chalecos salvavidas están en un bolsillo de bajo de cada asiento en la cabina.

Su chaleco salvavidas se infla fácilmente y le mantendrá a flote pase lo que pase. No remueva el chaleco salvavidas del saco sellado hasta que sea necesario, ya que éste ha sido inspeccionado y sellado en el saco para asegurar su mejor funcionamiento.

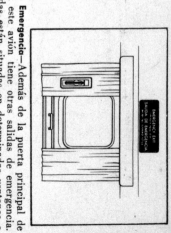

COMO PONERSE SU CHALECO SALVAVIDAS

(A) Póngase el chaleco salvavidas sobre su cabeza.

(B) Abroche las hebillas; ajústelo alrededor de la cintura.

(C) DESPUES QUE HA SALIDO DEL AVION, tire con fuerza de los cordones para inflarlo.

(D) Si luego el chaleco empezara a desinflarse, usted puede soplarlo con la boca.

EN CASO DE AMARIZAJE DE EMERGENCIA

Permanezca sereno y siga las instrucciones de la tripulación.

Agarre su chaleco salvavidas y póngaselo.

Coloque el espaldar de su asiento en posición vertical y amárrese el cinturon de seguridad.

Siéntese en posición para amarizaje de emergencia, inclínese hacia adelante, baje la cabeza y colóquela entre las piernas, enlace las manos abarcando por debajo de las piernas, manteniendo los músculos en tensión.

Cuando el avión se haya detenido totalmente, suéltese el cinturon de seguridad. Infle su chaleco salvavidas *solamente después que haya abandonado la nave.* Siga las instrucciones de la tripulación para abandonar la nave y abordar la balsa salvavidas.

Esta nave se mantiene en contacto frecuente y regular por radio con el Departamento de Control de Vuelo de la Eastern. En caso de emergencia, las facilidades de rescate y salvamiento se pondrán inmediatamente en acción.

Balsas Salvavidas—Hay abordo suficientes balsas salvavidas con capacidad para 20 personas cada una, para acomodar a todas los pasajeros y a los miembros de la tripulación en caso de emergencia. En todo momento los miembros de la tripulación, quienes han sido debidamente adiestrados para cualquier emergencia, inflarán y botarán al agua las balsas salvavidas. Estas balsas están equipadas con provisiones de emergencia, equipo de primeros auxilios, etc.

LOCALIZACION DE LAS BALSAS SALVAVIDAS Y SALIDAS DE EMERGENCIA

Los círculos indican el número de balsas salvavidas situadas en determinada posición. Las flechas señalan las salidas de emergencia.

Salidas de Emergencia—Además de la puerta principal de la cabina, este avión tiene otras salidas de emergencia. Estas salidas están situadas en determinadas ventanas a ambos lados de la cabina, debidamente identificadas. Para abrir estas salidas:

1. Múdese la lámina que cubre el mango de salida.
2. Hálese el mango de salida rojo hacia adentro y abajo.
3. Agárrese el mango de salida desde abajo y hálese hacia la cabina.

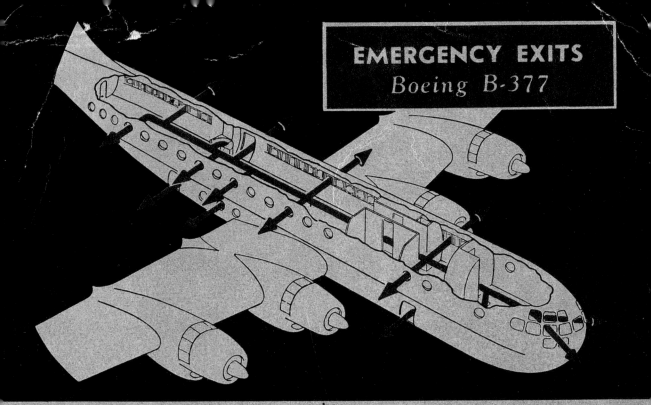

EMERGENCY EXITS
Boeing B-377

EMERGENCY EXITS AND EMERGENCY EQUIPMENT	SORTIES ET EQUIPMENT DE SECOURS

1. THE EMERGENCY EXITS CONSIST OF FUSELAGE ACCESS DOORS AND SPECIAL WINDOWS LOCATED AS SHOWN IN THE DIAGRAM ABOVE. JUST ABOVE EACH OF THESE WINDOWS IS A PLACARDED COVER PLATE WHICH CAN BE EASILY PULLED OFF. UNDER THIS PLATE IS A RED HANDLE WHICH WHEN PULLED RELEASES A PANEL CONTAINING THE WINDOW, THUS PROVIDING A LARGE SQUARE OPENING. IN CASE OF LANDING ON WATER USE UPPER DECK EXITS ONLY, KEEP LOWER DECK EXITS CLOSED.

2. YOUR LIFE JACKET IS LOCATED IN A ZIPPERED COMPARTMENT IN THE BACK OF THE SEAT IN FRONT OF YOU, EXCEPT FOR THE FOLLOWING CASES. IF YOU ARE IN THE SMALL FORWARD PASSENGER COMPARTMENT YOUR JACKET IS IN A COMPARTMENT AT THE FORWARD END OF THE UPPER BUNK. IF YOU ARE IN THE FIRST ROW OF SEATS IN THE MAIN CABIN YOUR JACKET IS IN A SIMILAR COMPARTMENT AT THE FORWARD END OF THE BUNK ABOVE YOU. IF YOU ARE IN THE FIRST ROW OF SEATS DIRECTLY BEHIND THE SPIRAL STAIRCASE YOUR JACKET IS IN A COMPARTMENT DIRECTLY IN FRONT OF YOU.
SPARE LIFE JACKETS ARE STOWED IN THE CABINET JUST TO THE RIGHT OF THE DOOR AS YOU COME ABOARD.

3. THE LIFE RAFTS ARE STOWED IN A CABINET ON THE WALL JUST TO THE RIGHT OF THE DOOR AS YOU COME ABOARD.

4. THERE ARE FOUR FIRE EXTINGUISHERS IN THE PASSENGER COMPARTMENTS OF THE AIRPLANE, ONE AT THE ENTRANCE TO THE LADIES' POWDER ROOM, ONE AT THE REAR OF THE AIRPLANE UNDER THE LAST SEAT ON THE RIGHT-HAND SIDE (LOOKING FORWARD), ONE IN THE COCKTAIL LOUNGE LOCKER AT THE BOTTOM OF THE SPIRAL STAIRWAY, AND ONE ON THE SPIRAL STAIRWAY SUPPORT COLUMN IN THE COCKTAIL LOUNGE.

5. THE FIRST-AID KIT IS IN THE SMALL COAT RACK AT THE REAR OF THE AIRPLANE BEHIND THE LAST ROW OF SEATS ON THE LEFT HAND SIDE (LOOKING FORWARD).

1. Les *SORTIES DE SECOURS* se composent des portes d'accès au fuselage et des hublots spéciaux disposés comme le montre le diagramme ci-dessus. Chacun de ces hublots est surmonté d'une plaque recouvrante placardée, qu'on peut facilement retirer. Sous cette plaque il y a une manette rouge qui, une fois tirée, dégage un panneau contenant le hublot, en procurant ainsi une grande ouverture carrée. En cas d'amerrissage, servez-vous uniquement des sorties du pont supérieur et laissez fermées les sorties du pont inférieur.

2. Le dos du siège devant vous est muni d'un compartiment à fermeture éclair, qui contient votre *GILET DE SAUVETAGE*. Cependant, il y a les exceptions suivantes: Pour les passagers du compartiment avant, les gilets se trouvent dans un compartiment pratiqué dans la partie avant de la couchette supérieure. Pour les occupants de la première rangée de sièges de la cabine principale, les gilets se trouvent dans un compartiment semblable pratiqué dans la partie avant de la couchette au-dessus d'eux. Ceux qui occupent la première rangée de sièges derrière l'escalier tournant, trouvent leurs gilets dans un compartiment juste devant eux.
A droite de la porte d'accès à la cabine se trouve un placard contenant des gilets des sauvetage supplémentaires.

3. Dans le placard contenant les gilets des sauvetage supplémentaires (voir 2) se trouvent les *RADEAUX DE SAUVETAGE*.

4. Les compartiments des passagers sont munis de quatre *EXTINCTEURS* disposés comme suit: 1) à l'entrée du cabinet pour dames; 2) dans la partie arrière de l'avion sous le dernier siège à droite (en regardant vers l'avant); 3) dans le coffre du bar en bas de l'escalier tournant; 4) sur le mur de l'escalier dans le bar.

5. La *PHARMACIE PORTATIVE* se trouve dans le petit porte-manteaux de la partie arrière de l'avion, derrière la dernière rangée de sièges à gauche (en regardant vers l'avant).

PAN AMERICAN WORLD AIRWAYS
The System of the Flying Clippers

9241-0048

EMERGENCY LANDING INSTRUCTIONS
Instructions Pour Atterrissage d'Urgence

KEEP CALM. THE CAPTAIN AND THE CREW KNOW EXACTLY WHAT TO DO IN ANY EVENTUALITY, AND YOU WILL RECEIVE SPECIFIC INSTRUCTIONS ACCORDINGLY. NO ACTION SHOULD BE TAKEN ON YOUR PART UNLESS THUS DIRECTED.

Ne perdez pas votre sang-froid. En toutes circonstances, le Commandant et l'équipage sont parfaitement au courant des mesures à prendre et vous donneront des instructions précises. Abandonnez toute initiative personnelle et conformez-vous aux instructions reçues.

REMEMBER THAT WHILE THE CAPTAIN MAY HAVE PLAYED THE GENIAL HOST UNDER NORMAL CONDITIONS, HIS AUTHORITY IS ABSOLUTE AT ALL TIMES. UNDER EMERGENCY CONDITIONS HE CAN BROOK NO COMPROMISE OR QUESTION FROM EITHER PASSENGERS OR CREW. COOPERATE QUICKLY AND QUIETLY TO AVOID CONFUSION.

Si bon hôte que soit le Commandant quand les circonstances sont normales, n'oubliez pas que son autorité est absolue et suprême. En cas d'urgence, il ne tolère aucune immixtion de la part des passagers et de l'équipage. Par conséquent, pour éviter la confusion, donnez-lui toute coopération et obéissez tranquillement et promptement à ses ordres.

LOOSEN YOUR COLLAR AND TIE. REMOVE GLASSES AND SHARP OBJECTS FROM YOUR POCKETS, BUT KEEP ALL YOUR CLOTHES ON.

Desserrez votre col et dénouez votre cravate. Retirez de vos poches tous objets tranchants ainsi que les lunettes, mais n'ôtez pas vos vêtements.

WHEN SO ORDERED, BUT NOT BEFORE, PUT ON YOUR LIFE JACKET. AT THIS TIME YOU WILL BE SHOWN HOW TO PUT IT ON, AND GIVEN ADEQUATE INSTRUCTIONS IN ITS USE.

Mettez le gilet de sauvetage après en avoir reçu l'ordre, mais pas avant. Des instructions vous seront données pour le revêtir et pour en faire usage.

ADJUST YOUR SEAT BACK TO THE VERTICAL POSITION AND FASTEN YOUR SAFETY BELT AS TIGHTLY AS POSSIBLE.

Ramenez votre siège à la position verticale et serrez la ceinture de sécurité autant que possible.

JUST BEFORE LANDING BRACE YOURSELF BY CLASPING YOUR HANDS UNDER YOUR KNEES, AND BEND FORWARD WITH YOUR HEAD BETWEEN YOUR KNEES OR AS NEARLY SO AS POSSIBLE.

Au moment où l'avion va atterrir, joignez les mains sous les genoux et inclinez la tête aussi bas que possible vers les genoux.

AS SOON AS THE AIRCRAFT HAS COME TO REST, ONE OF THE PLANE'S OFFICERS WILL ISSUE INSTRUCTIONS FOR LEAVING THE AIRCRAFT AND ENTERING THE LIFE RAFTS (IF THE LANDING IS AT SEA). HE IS THE CAPTAIN'S REPRESENTATIVE AND IS IN COMPLETE AUTHORITY.

Dès l'atterrissage, un des officiers du bord donnera aux passagers des instructions pour descendre de l'avion ou, en cas d'amerissage, pour se rendre aux radeaux de sauvetage. Etant le représentant du Commandant, il est investi d'autorité complète.

89TH MILITARY AIRLIFT WING
MILITARY AIRLIFT COMMAND, USAF

IMPORTANT INFORMATION

It's very unlikely that your MAC plane, manned by skilled and experienced pilots and crew, will ever have to "ditch," as landing on water is called. But it's a good idea for you to know about the safety measures we've provided.

OVER WATER FLIGHT PROCEDURES

EMERGENCY EXITS (Ditching)

The VC-118A is adequately equipped with emergency facilities. Emergency exits are illustrated on the diagram. Near the center of the cabin are four removable window exits. Placards are at each exit, giving simple and clear instructions as to their use in the event of an emergency. One exit door is located in the forward cabin and one in the rear cabin. All exits are marked by arrows on the diagram.

GETTING READY

If you are given the order to "prepare for ditching," empty your pockets of all sharp objects such as pencils, take off your glasses, and remove your tie. Take off highheeled shoes.

IT'S EASY TO PUT ON YOUR LIFE VEST

A life vest is provided for each passenger. You'll be shown where it is. To put it on:

1. Remove the vest from carrying bag. Slip arms through shoulder harness and buckle chest strap.

2. Bring vest up snugly under armpits by pulling down on shoulder harness adjustment straps.

3. Tighten vest snugly by pulling on chest adjustment strap.

4. As you leave the airplane inflate vest by pulling sharply on the two lanyards (red tabs) at bottom front of vest.

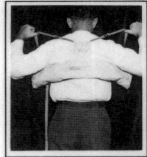

IN CASE OF AN EMERGENCY LANDING ON WATER

A After your life vest is on, put your seat forward in an upright position, and fasten your seat belt.

B Lean forward, rest your head on your knees, and hold a blanket, a pillow or clothing over your head as a cushion against impact.

C When the plane has come to a complete stop, unfasten your seat belt. Wait for a crew member's instructions for leaving the airplane and stepping into the life raft.

D Inflate your life vest only as you leave the airplane. A crew member will tell you when.

E Radio communications have already started rescue on its way.

There are emergency exits in this airplane which are clearly marked. Your crew will show them to you. Please do not leave your seat before the airplane has come to a complete stop. The pilots and crew have been thoroughly trained in the use of the rescue equipment on board. All you have to do is follow their instructions carefully and help them and yourself by keeping calm.

WINDOW EXITS

1. Hook fingers in plastic shield over RED handle — pull off.
2. Lift RED handle up.
3. Push window outward.

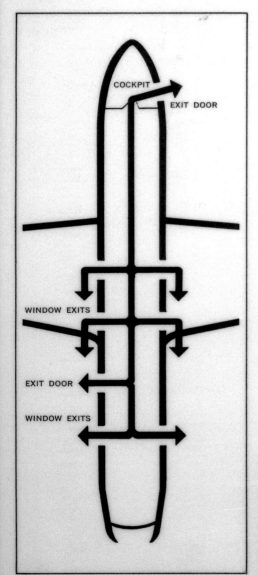

COCKPIT

EXIT DOOR

WINDOW EXITS

EXIT DOOR

WINDOW EXITS

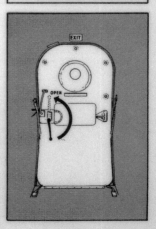

IMPORTANT INFORMATION

GROUND EVACUATION PROCEDURES

DOOR EXIT

1. TURN DOOR HANDLE UP.
2. PUSH DOOR OUT — CREW MEMBER WILL ATTACH SLIDE.

WINDOW EXITS

1. HOOK FINGERS IN PLASTIC SHIELD OVER **RED** HANDLE — PULL OFF.
2. LIFT **RED** HANDLE UP.
3. PUSH WINDOW OUTWARD.

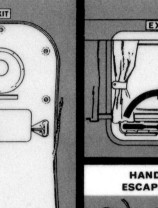

HAND HELD ESCAPE SLIDE

BRACE POSITION

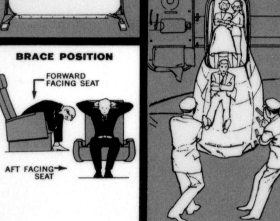

GROUND EVACUATION EMERGENCY EXITS

The VC-118A is adequately equipped with emergency facilities. Emergency exits are illustrated on the diagram. Near the center of the cabin are four removable window exits. Placards are at each exit, giving simple and clear instructions as to their use in the event of an emergency. One exit door is located in the forward cabin and one in the rear cabin. All exits are marked by arrows on the diagram. The exit doors are equipped with rapid evacuation slides.

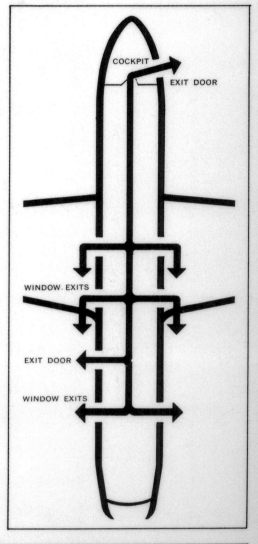

RADIO RECEIVERS AND ELECTRONIC DEVICES

Operating portable radios, cordless razors and other electronic devices (except hearing aids) is prohibited aboard this aircraft. Some electronic devices act as miniature broadcast stations, strong enough to interfere with the aircraft navigation system. Ask your cabin attendant about approved outlets for your electric razor.

SEAT BELTS

Move around as much as you like in the Cabin while the seat belt sign is off. We suggest, however, that you keep your seat belt loosely fastened while in your seats. Of course, seat belts must be fastened any time the seat belt sign is on.

SMOKING AND CIGARETTE LIGHTERS

When the "NO SMOKING" sign is off, you may smoke cigarettes while seated anywhere in the cabin or stateroom. Whenever the "NO SMOKING" sign comes on, however, ALL smokes are to be extinguished. Please observe the "NO SMOKING" sign. For your safety, cigarette lighters fueled with butane gas or having a see-through plastic reservoir, must not be used aboard this aircraft. Although not used, any lighter may cause painful chemical burns if fuel leakage is permitted to make prolonged contact with the skin.

PLEASE DO NOT TAKE THIS CARD FROM THE AIRCRAFT   PLEASE SEE REVERSE SIDE

Belgian air lines

CONSIGNES D'AMERRISSAGE FORCÉ EN

DITCHING PROCEDURE WITH

NOODLANDING OP ZEE MET

DOUGLAS DC·6

GROUP 1

GROUP 3

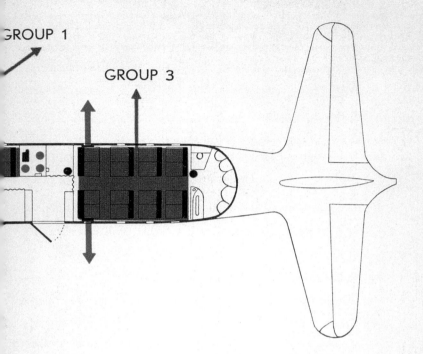

Belgian air lines

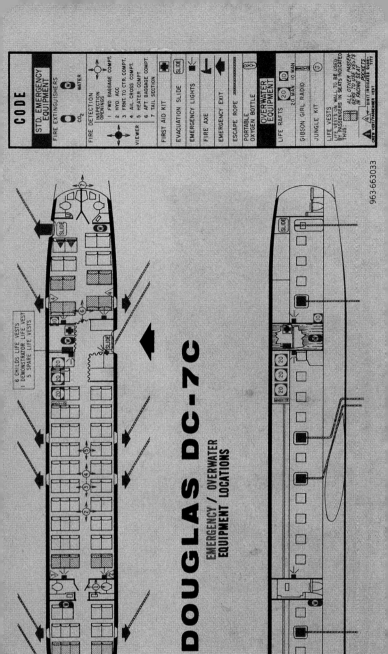

DOUGLAS DC-7C
EMERGENCY / OVERWATER EQUIPMENT LOCATIONS

CODE

STD. EMERGENCY EQUIPMENT

FIRE EXTINGUISHERS
CO_2 WATER

FIRE DETECTION
INSPECTION OPENINGS
1 FWD BAGGAGE COMPT.
2 HYD ACC
3 FRNT. TO CTR. COMPT.
4 AIL. CROSS COMPT.
5 HEATER COMPT
6 AFT. BAGGAGE COMPT
7 TAIL SECTION

VIEWER

FIRST AID KIT

EVACUATION SLIDE   SLIDE

EMERGENCY LIGHTS

FIRE AXE

EMERGENCY EXIT

ESCAPE ROPE

PORTABLE OXYGEN BOTTLE

OVERWATER EQUIPMENT

LIFE RAFTS   20
20 MAN 10 MAN

GIBSON GIRL RADIO

JUNGLE KIT

LIFE VESTS
LIFE VESTS ON WALL TO BE USED BY PASSENGERS IN SEATS INDICATED THUS: ALL OTHER PASSENGERS TO USE VESTS IN FACING SEAT.
DEMO. VEST/PASSENGER QUAN.   CHILD VEST

6 CHILDS LIFE VESTS
1 DEMONSTRATOR LIFE VEST
5 SPARE LIFE VESTS

963-663033

OVER-WATER FLIGHT INFORMATION

The aircraft in which you are flying is one of the most modern and dependable planes in the world. While there is little likelihood that we will have to land on the water, we would like to acquaint you with the aircraft's safety equipment.

LIFE VESTS are provided for all passengers and crew members. These vests are easily inflated and will keep you afloat and upright under any circumstances. Do not inflate life vests inside the cabin.

LIFE RAFTS, capable of holding all passengers and crew members, are well equipped with supplies and rations. Do not inflate life rafts inside the cabin.

EMERGENCY EXITS, located at certain windows throughout the cabin, are clearly indicated and labeled with easy opening instructions. The location of the above facilities is shown on the reverse side.

WHAT TO DO IN CASE OF A WATER LANDING

Your crew has been thoroughly trained in the use of all emergency equipment. Follow their instructions carefully. Place the back of your seat in an upright position and fasten your seat belt tightly across your lap. Remove all sharp objects from your pockets. Just prior to actual landing on the water, lean forward with the side of your head resting on a pillow; embrace your legs with your arms. After the aircraft has come to a *complete stop*, unfasten your seat belt. Follow the crew's instructions for leaving the aircraft and boarding the life rafts. Please wait to inflate your life vest until you have left the aircraft.

Our aircraft maintain constant radio contact with our flight control center, and our position is always known. Should we have to make a water landing, rescue operations would be started immediately.

INFORMACION CONCERNIENTE AL PROGRESO DEL VUELO SOBRE EL MAR

La aeronave en la cual Ud. está volando es una de las más modernas y seguras del mundo. Aunque las posibilidades de que el avión tenga que acuatizar son muy remotas, queremos que Ud. esté familiarizado con el equipo de seguridad que este avión posee.

CHALECOS SALVAVIDAS: Los hay a disposición de todos los pasajeros y de los miembros de la tripulación. Estos chalecos son fáciles de inflar y lo mantendrán a Ud. a flote y en posición vertical, bajo cualquier circunstancia. Se ruega el favor de no inflar el chaleco mienrtas Ud. se encuentre dentro de la cabina.

BOTES SALVAVIDAS: Los hay en cantidad suficiente para acomodar a todos los pasajeros y a los miembros de la tripulación y están provistos de alimentos y de equipo especial. Se ruega el favor de no inflar los botes mientras Ud. se encuentre dentro de la cabina.

SALIDAS DE EMERGENCIA: Están colocadas en algunas de las ventanas a todo lo largo de la cabina. Están indicadas con claridad y llevan un rótulo con las instrucciones sobre su manejo, muy fáciles de entender y seguir.

QUE HACER EN CASO DE "ACUATIZAJE"

La tripulación está ampliamente entrenada en el manejo del equipo de emergencia. Siga cuidadosamente las instrucciones que los triplantes le impartan.

Coloque el espaldar de su asiento en posición completamente vertical y abróchese el cinturon de seguridad bien ajustado. Saque de sus bolsillos todos los objetos punzantes.

Momentos antes de "acuatizar," incline el cuerpo hacia adelante, apoyando la cabeza de medio lado sobre una almohada y trate de ceñirse las piernas con los brazos.

Cuando el avión haya detenido su marcha en forma definitiva, desabróchese el cinturón de seguridad y siga las instrucciones que le imparta la tripulación, a fin de abandonar la aeronave y ocupar los botes salvavidas.

Se ruega el favor de inflar el chaleco salvavidas unicamente cuando Ud. se encuentre fuera de la cabina.

BRANIFF *International* AIRWAYS

IMPORTANT INFORMATION
FOR VISCOUNT II PASSENGERS

We want you to know about certain safety features of the Viscount II.

CONTINENTAL AIRLINES

EMERGENCY EXITS

Nine exits are provided for your use. One on right side forward section, six at mid section over wing area and two rear door exits located in rear of plane. The chart below shows their locations. All emergency windows are so marked by an illuminated sign above the window. The emergency windows may be opened by: (1) Push back of forward seat to incline it forward. (2) Lift up on Red flap over handle above the window. (3) Pull out on the release handle found beneath this flap until you feel it release. (4) Pull in on the handle on the top side of the window itself. The two emergency door exits are equipped with slide chutes as shown on reverse side of this card.

FOR ADDITIONAL INFORMATION ASK YOUR CABIN ATTENDANT

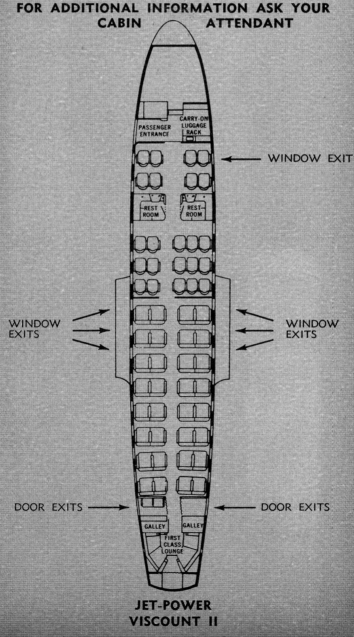

JET-POWER VISCOUNT II

See Other Side →

EVACUATION SLIDE DIAGRAM

Located in floor of the two emergency door exits in rear of plane.

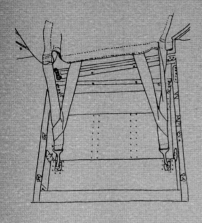

1. Push latches in floor to open door.

2. Hook the red and green hooks into corresponding colored door sill openings.

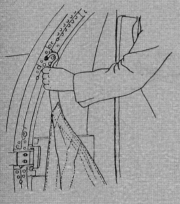

3. Throw loose end of chute out of entrance door. Lower end of chute is permanently fastened into floor. Close slide compartment door.

4. Two male passengers will slide down the slide to ground.

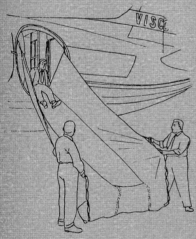

1. Hold chute by grasping handles on side of chute at the correct length.

2. Hold very taut.

3. Passengers should remove shoes.

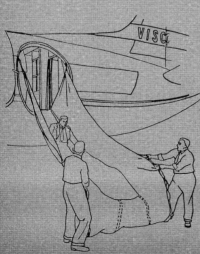

1. Passengers will sit in door sill on chute.

2. Hostess will push passenger out.

See Other Side →

Sorry, this seat is

OCCUPIED

thank you OZARK AIR LINES

OZARK ⇒ ⇒ ⇒

AIRCRAFT EMERGENCY EXITS

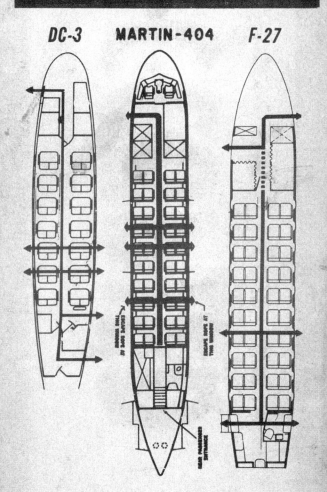

DC-3   MARTIN-404   F-27

Sorry

THIS SEAT IS

OCCUPIED

ALLEGHENY AIRLINES

DO NOT REMOVE FROM AIRCRAFT

ALLEGHENY AIRLINES
EMERGENCY EXITS

The Martin Aircraft on which you are traveling is one of the safest aircraft in service today. One of its safety features is its emergency exits which we would like to tell you about.

—There are six emergency window exits, marked on the diagram below with black arrows. Each window has an escape rope in the upper frame or under the seat.

—The door at the rear of the cabin is also an emergency exit. It is marked on the diagram below with a gray arrow.

—The cargo door at the front of the aircraft is also an emergency exit. It is marked on the diagram below with a gray arrow. This door has an evacuation slide. An escape rope is next to the door.

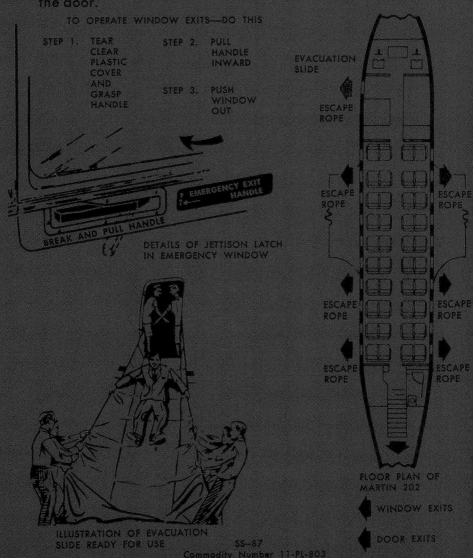

TO OPERATE WINDOW EXITS—DO THIS

STEP 1. TEAR CLEAR PLASTIC COVER AND GRASP HANDLE

STEP 2. PULL HANDLE INWARD

STEP 3. PUSH WINDOW OUT

EMERGENCY EXIT HANDLE

BREAK AND PULL HANDLE

DETAILS OF JETTISON LATCH IN EMERGENCY WINDOW

EVACUATION SLIDE

ESCAPE ROPE

ESCAPE ROPE

ESCAPE ROPE

ESCAPE ROPE

ESCAPE ROPE

ESCAPE ROPE

ESCAPE ROPE

FLOOR PLAN OF MARTIN 202

WINDOW EXITS

DOOR EXITS

ILLUSTRATION OF EVACUATION SLIDE READY FOR USE

SS—87
Commodity Number 11-PL-803

please read carefully

This is your

Safety Leaflet

B·O·A·C takes good care of you

BRITISH OVERSEAS AIRWAYS CORPORATION

56/313/50M/KHK   (Lightweight)   Printed in Great Britain

IMPORTANT INFORMATION

EMERGENCY BRIEFING CARD

SANDRINGHAM ——————————————— VH – BRF

Your safety is our first consideration and every possible precaution is taken to ensure it. These instructions are for your guidance in the unlikely event of an emergency occurring. Rough air at high altitudes, although infrequent, can be severe. We strongly recommend that your seat belt be fastened at all times and pulled tight whenever the seat belt sign is on.

LIFE JACKETS

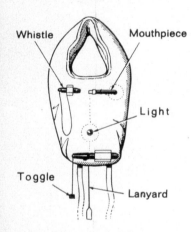

Whistle   Mouthpiece

Light

Toggle

Lanyard

Your life jacket is located underneath your seat.

1. Remove the jacket from container.
2. Pass the jacket over your head.
3. Tie the tapes securely around your waist underneath the life jacket.
4. When instructed, pull the red toggle firmly downward to inflate.

If necessary, use the mouthpiece afterwards for further inflation.
To operate the light, pull the lanyard downward until completely detached.
You must not inflate your life jacket whilst you are inside the aircraft.

BRACE POSITION

1. Straighten seat back vertically.
2. Tighten your seat belt.
3. Remove glasses, dentures and any sharp articles which could cause injury in a sudden jolt.
4. When instructed, assume brace position as illustrated.
5. Do not move until aircraft finally comes to rest.

PLEASE DO NOT REMOVE THIS CARD FROM AIRCRAFT

ANSETT PART NO. 250   PRINTED IN AUSTRALIA

LOCATION OF EMERGENCY EXITS AND INSTRUCTIONS FOR OPENING

WINDOW EXITS

KNOCK-OUT

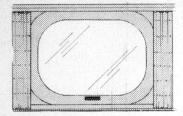

Give a sharp blow to one edge of window with foot or hand.

UPPER CABIN (REAR)

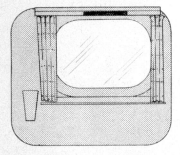

Lift flap, turn handle and push window.

TOILET AND GALLEY

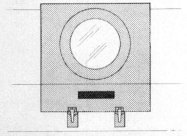

Press catches and pull window inwards.

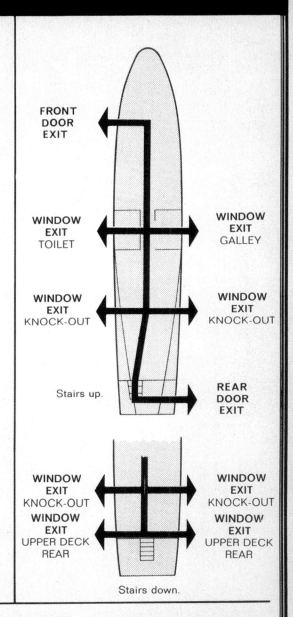

FRONT DOOR EXIT

WINDOW EXIT TOILET

WINDOW EXIT GALLEY

WINDOW EXIT KNOCK-OUT

WINDOW EXIT KNOCK-OUT

Stairs up.

REAR DOOR EXIT

WINDOW EXIT KNOCK-OUT

WINDOW EXIT KNOCK-OUT

WINDOW EXIT UPPER DECK REAR

WINDOW EXIT UPPER DECK REAR

Stairs down.

DOOR EXITS

REAR   FRONT

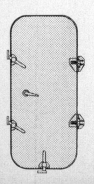

Turn handles in the appropriate directions. Pull door inward.

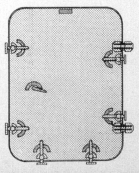

PLEASE DO NOT REMOVE THIS CARD FROM AIRCRAFT

ÖRYGGI UM BORÐ
SAFETY ON BOARD

BJÖRGUNARVESTIÐ

er í poka undir sæti yðar. Það má fylla lofti með því að toga í snúruna sem liggur að kolsýrugeymi eða blása í stútinn, sem því er tengdur. En þetta á aldrei að gera inni í flugvélinni, því að sá, sem er í útblásnu vesti verður svo fyrirferðarmikill, að honum myndi ganga erfiðlega að komast út um neyðarútganginn sem auðkenndur er með orðunum EMERGENCY EXIT.

THE LIFE JACKET

is in a pocket under your seat. It can be inflated by pulling a cord which leads to a carbon dioxide container, or by blowing into the mouthpiece which is attached to it, but this should never be done inside the aircraft, for after the life jacket has been inflated, it becomes so bulky that the person wearing it would have difficulty in getting through the safety doors of the aircraft, which are marked by the words EMERGENCY EXIT.

BJÖRGUNARBÁTARNIR

Ef nauðlent er á sjó mun áhöfn flugvélarinnar koma út þeim björgunarbátum, sem jafnan eru í flugvélinni, en þeir eru traustir og burðarmiklir. Í bátunum eru vistir og margvísleg öryggistæki. Þar sem flugvélarnar haldast oft alllengi ofansjávar, eftir að þeim hefir verið lent, er skynsamlegt að fara rólega og æðrulaust um borð í björgunarbátana og hlýða fyrirskipunum flugliðanna, sem annast stjórn þeirra, en þeir hafa fengið sérstaka þjálfun í því og eru af þeim sökum færir um að leiðbeina og nota réttilega þau tæki, sem eru í bátunum.

SAFETY AT SEA

In case of an emergency landing on the water, the crew of the aircraft will launch the liferafts, which are always kept in readiness. The rafts are seaworthy and with great buoyancy. They are equipped with food and various safety devices. As the aircraft usually keeps above water for a considerable length of time after landing, it is wisest to board the liferafts calmly and quietly, and obey the orders given by the crew members in charge. They are specially trained in this practice, and for that reason they are capable of giving proper instructions and handling the equipment in the rafts.

TAKIÐ VESTIÐ ÚR POKANUM
REMOVE JACKET FROM VALISE

SMEYGIÐ VESTINU YFIR HÖFUÐ
PASS JACKET OVER HEAD

BINDIÐ SNÚRUNA UM MITTIÐ
TIE TAPES ROUND WAIST

TOGIÐ Í SNÚRUNA MEÐ RAUÐA HNÚÐNUM
INFLATE BY PULLING RED TOGGLE

BÆTIÐ VIÐ LOFTI EÐA FYLLIÐ Á NÝ MEÐ ÞVÍ AÐ BLÁSA Í MUNNSTYKKIÐ
REINFLATE OR TOP-UP USING MOUTHPIECE

TOGIÐ Í SNÚRUNA MEÐ GULA MIÐANUM. ÞÁ LOSNA TAPPARNIR OG LJÓSIÐ TENDRAST
ILLUMINATE LIGHT BY PULLING TAP AND REMOVING CORD COMPLETELY

LÁTIÐ ENNI HVÍLA Á HANDLEGGJUM, KROSSLÖGÐUM YFIR HNJÁM
LET FOREHEAD REST ON ARMS IN A CROSS POSITION OVER KNEES

ÖRYGGI UM BORÐ

Allt hofir verið gert, sem unnt er, til þess að tryggja öryggi yðar og ánægju í ferðalaginu. Áður en ferðin var hafin fullvissuðu kunnáttumenn sig um, að flug-vélin væri vel búin undir langa ferð. Áhöfnin hefir að baki sér langa þjálfun og reynslu, og sérfræðingar í flugstöðvunum fylgjast með ferð hennar. Alls konar öryggistæki eru í flugvélinni, og þetta spjald er gert til þess að leiðbeina yður um rétta notkun sumra þeirra.

SAFETY ON BOARD

Everything possible is done that your voyage may be a comfortable and a safe one. Before the voyage was commenced, specialists made sure that the aircraft was well prepared for a long flight. Its crew is well trained and with a long experience, and specialists at our stations keep in touch with the flight. Every kind of safety equipment is to be found in the air-craft, and this information has been compiled to in-struct you in the correct use of some of it.

ÖRYGGISRÁÐSTAFANIR VEGNA NAUÐLENDINGAR

Ef til þess kynni að koma, að flugstjóri tæki ákvörð-un um nauðlendingu, sem hann tilkynnir þá með orð-unum PREPARE FOR EMERGENCY LANDING (Undirbú-ið yður vegna nauðlendingar), þá ber farþegum að losa um hálsbindi og flibba, fara úr hælaháum skóm, fjarlægja gleraugu, gervitennur, nálar og blýanta, taka pokann með vestinu, fara í björgunarvestið eins og sýnt er með skýringarmyndum, en fylla það EKKI með lofti, spenna sig þannig með sætisólunum, að þær séu festar yfir mjaðmir, og bíða svo nánari fyrir-mæla áhafnarinnar.

Önnur fyrirskipun, sem gefin verður rétt fyrir nauð-lendingu er þessi: READY FOR EMERGENCY LANDING (Verið viðbúin: Nauðlending). Þá ber farþegum að láta enni hvila á handleggjum, sem krosslagðir eru yfir knjám, en þannig skal bíða, unz flugvélin stöðv-ast að fullu. Tveir rykkir gefa venjulega til kynna, að flugvélin sé lent, hinn síðari harkalegri þeim fyrri. Þegar flugvélin stöðvast á að losa öryggisbelti og leita þeirra neyðardyra, sem flugliðar vísa á. Nauðsynlegt er að sýna fulla stillingu, fara að þeim fyrirmælum, sem áhöfnin gefur og fylla ekki björgunarvestið með lofti fyrr en komið er út úr flugvélinni.

SAFETY RULES FOR EMERGENCY LANDING

If the event the Captain of the aircraft should decide to make an emergency landing, which he would then announce by the words: PREPARE FOR EMERGENCY LANDING, the passengers should loosen collar and tie, take off high-heeled shoes, remove glasses, artificial teeth, pins and pencils, take the bag containing the life jacket, put on the life jacket as shown by the instructions, but it should NOT be in-flated; they should fasten themselves with the seat belt so that it is securely around the hips, and then await the crew's further orders.

The second order given just before an emergency landing is as follows: READY FOR EMERGENCY LAND-ING. Passengers should then rest the forhead on the arms folded over the knees, and thus they should wait until the aircraft finally comes to a standstill. Usually two bumps indicate that the aircraft has landed, the latter harder than the first. When the aircraft has come to a standstill, the safety belt should be released, and the safety door indicated by the crew, should be sought. It is necessary to keep absolutely calm and to follow the instructions given by the crew, and the life jacket should not be inflated until once outside the aircraft.

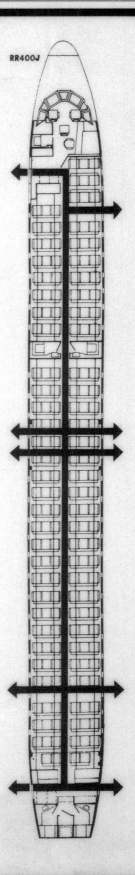

RR400J

Page 21. Lufthansa "Wasserlandung" (landing on water). Cards such as this one were used on the Lockhead Constellation in the mid-1950s.

Page 23. Lufthansa, Lockhead Constellation. Lufthansa's first commercial flight connected Hamburg and New York via Düsseldorf and Shannon, Ireland. Lufthansa operated the Super Constellation until 1967. This folded card is from the early 1960s.

Page 25. Qantas "safety procedures". These cards were used on the Lockhead Constellation in the mid-1950s.

Page 27. Air France, Lockhead Constellation. Air France used the "Connie" until 1967.

Page 29. Eastern Airlines, Lockhead Constellation. This card is from 1958.

Page 31. Pan Am, Boeing 377 Stratocruiser. These cards were used in the late 1950s, although some of them were still in use up until the aircraft was decommissioned in the early 1960s.

Page 33. Douglas VC-118A (military version of the DC-6), 89th military airlift wing. This is a safety card from the aircraft used by the United States presidency, the last presidential airplane to be powered by piston-driven engines. John F. Kennedy first used this aircraft in September 1961. It remained part of the presidential fleet during the Kennedy-Johnson administration, even though the White House had acquired a VC-137, the military version of Boeing 707, to be used as "Air Force One". The VC-118A remained in production until 1958 and many are still flying today.

Page 35. Belgian Airlines, Douglas DC-6. This card was used in the early 1950s. Belgian Airlines later became Sabena.

Page 37. Braniff International Airways, Douglas DC-7. This card is from the late 1950s or very early 1960s. Braniff later abandoned individual cards in favour of so-called "fleet cards", where all the airline's models were represented. The fleet cards were banned by the FAA in 1967.

Page 39. Continental Airlines, Vickers Viscount. This card is from the mid-1960s.

Page 41. Ozark Airlines, Douglas DC-3, Martin-404 and F-27. This card was used in the 1960s.

Page 43. Allegheny Airlines, Martin-202. This card is from the mid-1960s. Note the non-inflatable, hand-held escape slide. The M-202 never introduced inflatable slides before it was decommissioned.

Page 45. B.O.A.C. "safety leaflet", 1956. This was used on all international B.O.A.C. flights, regardless of aircraft type.

Page 47. ANSETT-ANA, Sandringham VH-BRF. This Australian card is from the early 1970s. It was used on one of the very last "large" flying boats. The aircraft operated on the route from Sydney to Norfolk Island, before the service was taken over by Qantas DC-4 in 1972, when a runway adequate enough to handle a land-based aircraft was built.

Page 49. Canadair, Loftleidir CL-44J. This card is from the late 1960s or early 1970s.

The jet age begins

With the introduction of jet aircraft in the late 1950s, air travel would change dramatically. No longer would passengers have to stand the tiresome noise and unreliability of propeller engines. Jet airplanes would transport them smoothly and swiftly to their destinations. As expressed in an advertisement for B.O.A.C. in the late 1950s:

Fly by B.O.A.C. and S.A.A. – 4 flights weekly to Johannesburg. South Africa in less than a day...by Comet jet airliner...air travel at its finest, fastest, smoothest...yet at no extra fare. Leave London after lunch on a Tuesday and arrive at Johannesburg the following afternoon...as rested as when you set out. Cruising in the Comet in the upper air...at 8 miles a minute...you'll find there is a complete lack of vibration...absolutely no travel fatigue...delicious complementary meals and mealtime drinks are served in flight...prompt attention is paid to your every need...no tips or extras – not even for the superb service. Via Rome, Cairo, Entebbe and Livingstone at no extra fare....

The appeal for the late-1950s traveller was immediate. But the Comet airliner – the first commercial jet airplane – soon got a bad reputation, after a series of bizarre accidents and incidents, due to fatigue in the construction. Moreover, the Comet lacked the appropriate fuel-range to cross the Atlantic non-stop. The required refuelling stop made the Comet insufficiently comfortable for the passengers and the cost inefficient for the operator. After two especially nasty Comet crashes, the project was put on hold for a couple of years, allowing its competitors to catch up.

Enter the Boeing 707. What the Comet Mk.4 lacked in range and reliability, the Boeing 707 possessed. Boeing had learned a great deal from De Havilland's mistakes with the Comet, and had taken more time developing the new plane. The 707 also had considerably better passenger capacity. And with Pan Am starting a transatlantic route with the 707 in October 1958, from New York to Paris, the Comet was soon discounted. As is so often the case, the pioneer had been beaten by its follower.

With the introduction of jet technology in the 1960s, two major changes occurred on safety cards – the depiction of oxygen systems and, more generally, a greater technical approach to representing passenger safety. KLM, and many other carriers, added a second card, which explained the passenger oxygen system. These cards were a supplement to the general "ditching" (landing on water) card. In many cases, particularly outside the U.S., floor plans and exit operations would not be discussed for many years to come. Passengers would read that exits "will be operated by members of the crew".

In order to save money, many airlines produced cards that incorporated safety for their entire fleet of airplanes on the same card – these are nowadays referred to by collectors as "fleet cards". They were mainly text with a few illustrations and, rather insanely, showed every floor plan of every aircraft. This source of confusion for the infrequent flyer would cost some passengers their lives and the cards were banned by the authorities in 1967.

The introduction of new technology meant that many unique items would appear on safety cards: hand-held, non-inflatable escape slides, ceiling-mounted slides on early Boeings and DC-8s, and even erroneous exit configurations. (National, KLM, Viasa and other DC-8 operators' cards showed only two over-wing exits when there were actually four!)

A classic safety error in early jet planes was a solid swing-door in the bulkheads between classes. After many people died unnecessarily in a crash at Denver, the bulkhead door was removed, as were the cards picturing it.

Despite its initial problems, jet travel proved itself to be more efficient, reliable and comfortable than the pre-jet way of flying. And its popularity rose even more when it became cheaper to fly. Even though an economy-class seat of the late 1950s had more space and leg-room than a modern-day business-class seat, the difference in passenger capacity was dramatic compared with that of the old propeller planes. The airline operators were jumping for joy, their optimism comparable to the recent hype about information technology. Boeing's slogan was "Brings people together", which bears a strong resemblance to that of the mobile phone manufacturer Nokia today – "Connecting people". The jet age had only just begun.

The Comet

De Havilland had the innovative spirit and vision to build the first commercial jet aircraft. Even if the Comet was not as epoch-making as initially predicted, it was, nevertheless, a huge step into a previously unknown territory. Never before had a commercial airplane been designed for such high cruise speeds at such high altitude. The engineers and designers – who, at the time, had no computers or calculators – were facing completely new problems in concepts, materials and production methods. Nearly all the components of the new aircraft were designed in the De Havilland offices in Britain.

Early safety cards used typical 1950s design, with few images and a lot of text. The Comet used B.O.A.C.'s somewhat unsophisticated fleet cards, dangerous enough in themselves without the additional hazard of the aircraft's bad design – the emergency exits were located over the wings, which happened to be where the engines were located, generating extreme levels of heat. The Comet included so many innovative elements that it speeded up the development of new radar systems and radio technology, essential to the plane's safe operation.

Sir Miles Thomas, chairman of B.O.A.C., had his first Comet flight in an unpressurized prototype in November 1949. Despite having to wear an oxygen mask, and the cruising height being limited to 7,620 metres (25,000 feet), Thomas was left convinced that ordering the Comet had been a wise move. He found the experience exhilarating and was confident that the aircraft would give his airline a strong commercial advantage.

The first commercial flight took place on 2 May 1952. A Comet named Yoke Peter set off with 33 passengers on the 10,820 km (6,724 mile) flight from London Heathrow to Johannesburg via Rome, Beirut, Khartoum, Entebbe and Livingstone, and completed the flight in just under 24 hours. Sir Miles Thomas had flown to Livingstone on an earlier training flight in order to meet Yoke Peter on its arrival on 3 May. Despite tight scheduling, it became apparent that the Comet was going to arrive too early but, after killing a little time by making gentle sweeping "S" turns, the plane arrived a mere three minutes ahead of schedule – the point had been made, but without embarrassing the reception party. The event was broadcast all over the world. The Comet made a huge impact upon the civil aviation scene as the public could readily see that journey times were drastically reduced – the greater the distance the more the saving. Passengers embraced the Comet.

Production of the modified Comet Mk.2 was already well underway with deliveries to B.O.A.C. expected within 18 months. Yet it was already clear that the new Comets could not help B.O.A.C. on its highly competitive North Atlantic routes, since the range of the Mk.2, with full payload and without refuelling, would be insufficient. The Mk.2 was no longer an economical proposition for B.O.A.C. – or for any other carrier.

The Mk.3, however, held great promise. It was essentially a Mk.2 extended by 0.9 metres (3 feet) and with more powerful Avon engines, more fuel capacity and a significantly greater range. But De Havilland decided that the Mk.3 should not go into production. A radical redesign was completed quickly and the Mk.3 became the Mk.4 – an airplane that suited B.O.A.C.'s needs admirably. B.O.A.C. immediately placed an order for 19 aircraft. The Mk.4 made its maiden flight on 27 April 1958.

B.O.A.C. announced tentative plans to operate an Australian service from February 1959, although this seemed a little ambitious at the time. Meanwhile, rumours began to circulate that Pan Am were planning to introduce their new Boeing 707-120 on the North Atlantic route – the question was when. B.O.A.C. immediately began feasibility studies to see how best it could counter this commercial threat. It was accepted, however, that to change plans at this late stage would disrupt the carefully prepared pre-service programme. Gradually, during the latter half of 1958, stories began to circulate that B.O.A.C. was, after all, planning to put Comets on the North Atlantic route, and, furthermore, that scheduled services could begin in December of that year. Then rumour had it that B.O.A.C. had revised its plans and that 14 November was now the date set for the great event, the change apparently due to Pan Am's decision to commence services on 16 November. Whether leaks of B.O.A.C.'s revised plans spurred Pan Am into moving their date for the inaugural jet service is not known. They did, however, promptly embark on a massive advertising campaign, announcing that the first transatlantic services with the Boeing 707 would commence on 24 October 1958.

B.O.A.C. hinted that they might begin services on 17 October, and that Comets would replace their existing daily Monarch services to New York from mid-November. Because of the prevailing winds, the westbound flight needed to refuel at Gander in Newfoundland. This was something the 707, with its superior range, would not have to do. The inaugural flight was completed in 8 hours 53 minutes (including a stop-over of 10 hours 5 minutes) at an average ground speed of 650 km (404 miles) per hour.

B.O.A.C. had succeeded, and the fact that their scheduled transatlantic services were the first must have been worth millions of pounds to the corporation through the publicity generated. B.O.A.C. were to claim in their advertising that they were the "first 'pure jet' service ever to cross the Atlantic", whereas Pan Am were to claim rightly that they operated the fastest transatlantic service. In November B.O.A.C. announced the inauguration of jet services to Canada from the following month, with a weekly flight from London to Montreal. It was also revealed that on the eastbound New York–London route, Mk.4 services had been averaging 6 hours 45 minutes with a non-stop crossing. However, shortly after this, the Boeing 707 set a new eastbound record, cutting the flight time to less than six hours.

The Comet Mk.4 obviously did not have the true transatlantic capability that the larger 707 and DC-8 had. The Comet was intended primarily for the old Empire and Far Eastern routes, and it was here that B.O.A.C. rapidly expanded its operation of jet aircraft. Services resumed to South Africa towards the end of 1959. Comets operated on the Tokyo route and Hong Kong, Singapore and Sydney were all added by the end of the year. Competition from the Comet was beginning to upset some airlines not yet operating jet planes, however. It was said that Japan Airlines were exerting pressure on all jet operators, including Pan Am, demanding increased landing fees. As a result, B.O.A.C. was considering the imposition of a £2 surcharge on Comet Mk.4 flights between Tokyo and Hong Kong, to offset these additional charges.

Almost exactly two years after B.O.A.C. began its transatlantic services, the Comet was withdrawn from the route. It simply did not have the range. In September 1964, however, Comets were to be brought back on transatlantic routes to meet an unexpectedly high demand for flights from Scotland. B.O.A.C. operated three extra services a week from Scotland during August and September. And Comets still crossed the South Atlantic. At Rio de Janeiro's Galeao airport the runway was specifically extended to make it suitable for Comet Mk.4 operations, and B.O.A.C. included a stop at Rio on its scheduled London–Santiago service.

Yet it was also in 1964 that B.O.A.C. announced that it was soon to dispose of some of its 19 Comets. There had been enquiries from other operators who were considering buying Mk.4s. B.O.A.C. also let it be known that it expected to have two, or possibly three, Comets surplus to requirements in 1965. In fact, it offered one second-hand for sale at an asking price of £600,000.

Over the next five years all of B.O.A.C.'s Comets were sold off. Thus ended B.O.A.C.'s association with the airplane it had sponsored and supported from 1946. It had shown faith in the Comet Mk.1 by placing advanced orders. It had shown faith too in De Havilland, after the Comet's much publicized accidents, by ordering the Mk.4. It was a pity that after a 23-year association, B.O.A.C. only had, in effect, the benefit of ten years operational service with the Comet.

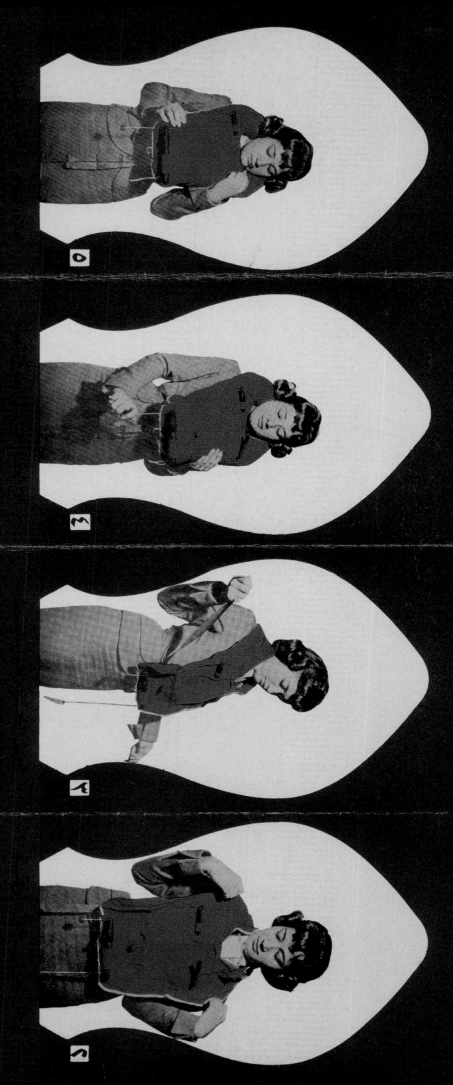

REMOVE LIFE JACKET FROM BAG

RETIRER LA SACT DE SIK

1

LIFEJACKET instructions

United Arab Airlines

BEA

Safety on board   **Comet**
Sécurité à bord
Sicherheit an bord

Emergency Exits · Sorties de secours · Notausgänge

Doors Portes Türen

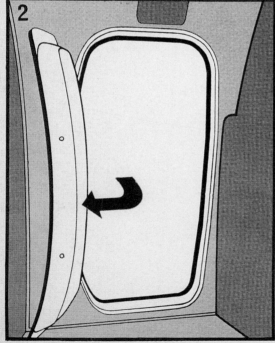

Windows Fenêtres Fenster

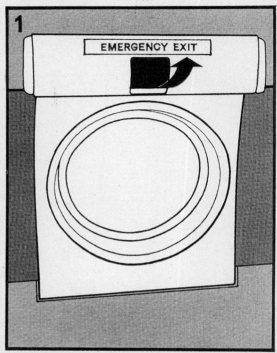

Printed in U.K. by I.A.L. (Aerad)

BEA Form No. F.349

BEA

Safety on board
Sécurité à bord
Sicherheit an bord

Comet

Safety Instructions

Your safety in our care is our first concern. Flying with a modern airline is safe but it is prudent that you should know what to do in any emergency, and we ask you to read this card carefully
In case of emergency, please obey implicitly the instructions of the crew, as they will often be able to direct you to a door or emergency exit which is nearer to your seat than the door by which you entered the aircraft.

Escape Slides

Escape slides are available by the main doors to enable passengers to reach the ground without the use of airport steps. If necessary, the operation will be supervised by the crew.

Consignes de sécurité

Votre sécurité est notre souci principal, tant que nous sommes à votre service. Le vol avec une compagnie aérienne moderne offre toute sécurité, mais il est prudent de savoir ce qu'il faut faire en cas d'urgence, et nous vous demandons de lire attentivement les indications suivantes sur la sécurité en vol.
En cas d'urgence, veuillez obéir aveuglément aux ordres des membres de l'équipage, car ils pourront souvent vous indiquer une porte ou sortie de secours qui se trouve plus près de votre siège que la porte par laquelle vous êtes entrés dans l'avion.

Rampes de Sauvetage

Les rampes de sauvetage se trouvent aux portes de sortie principales permettant aux passagers d atteindre le sol sans employer l'échelle de l'Aéroport.
Cette opération, en cas de besoin, ne sera effectuée que sous la surveillance de l'équipage.

Anweisungen für das Verhalten in Notfällen

Während Sie sich in unserer Obhut befinden, ist Ihre Sicherheit unser oberstes Gebot. Moderne Flugzeuge sind sicher, aber trotzdem sollten Sie wissen, wie man sich im Notfall verhält. Darum bitten wir Sie, diesen Abschnitt über Sicherheit gut durchzulesen.
Bei Gefahr befolgen Sie bitte genau die Anweisungen der Besatzung, da sie Ihnen oft einen Notausgang zeigen kann der Ihrem Sitz näher liegt als die Tür, durch die Sie das Flugzeug betraten.

Notrutsche

Die Passagier-Notrutschen befinden sich bei den Hauptausgängen, mit deren Hilfe Sie das Flugzeug ohne Treppe verlassen können. Sollte die Rutsche gebraucht werden, erfolgt dies unter Anleitung der Besatzung.

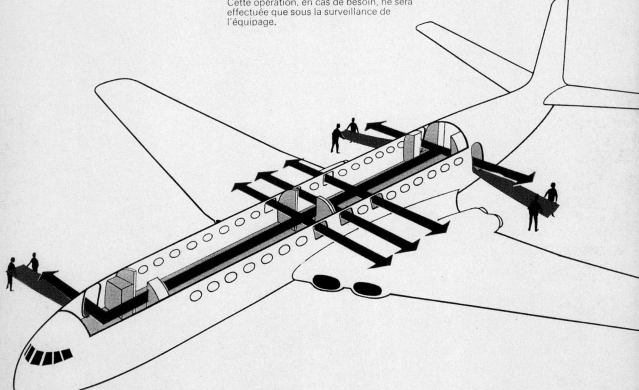

Emergency Landing Instructions

In the event of an emergency landing, the Captain will first of all announce 'Prepare for an emergency landing'. In this event please keep calm and carry out the following instructions:
1 Loosen neck wear, remove glasses, dentures and high-heeled shoes and empty pockets of sharp objects. Extinguish all cigarettes and do not use lighters or matches.
2 Ensure your seat back is in the vertical position and fasten your seat belt.

Continued over.

Instructions en cas d'atterrissage forcé

En cas d'atterrissage forcé, le Commandant annoncera tout d'abord 'Prepare for an emergency landing' (Préparez-vous pour un atterrissage forcé). Dans ce cas veuillez rester calme et suivre les instructions suivantes :
1 Desserrez vos vêtements autour du cou, enlevez vos lunettes, dentiers et chaussures à hauts talons, videz vos poches de tout objet pointu. Eteignez vos cigarettes et n'utilisez ni briquet ni allumettes.

Suite, verso.

Anweisungen für den Fall einer Notlandung

Wenn eine Notlandung bevorsteht, hören Sie zunächst die Durchsage des Kapitäns : "Prepare for an Emergency Landing". Bewahren Sie bitte Ruhe und verhalten Sie sich wie folgt :
1 Um den Hals getragene Kleidungsstücke lösen, Augengläser, künstliches Gebiss und Schuhe mit hohen Absätzen ablegen und scharfe Gegenstände aus den Taschen nehmen. Zigarette löschen. Feuerzeug und Streichhölzer nicht benutzen.

Fortsetzung Rückseite.

Please do not remove this card from aircraft.

MEXJET ROLLS ROYCE

PROCEDIMIENTOS DE SEGURIDAD

safety procedures

TOBOGAN DE ESCAPE

Los toboganes o "resbaladillas", de escape en éste avión, se encuentran instalados de la siguiente manera:

Frente a la puerta de entrada; en la puerta de salida de emergencia y en la puerta delantera de la tripulación. Estos toboganes fueron instalados con el objeto de que los pasajeros puedan salir deslizándose rápidamente del avión en caso de efectuarse un aterrizaje de emergencia. La tripulación ha sido debidamente adiestrada en su uso y sus instrucciones deberán seguirse sin vacilación.

EMERGENCY EXIT CHUTES

The chutes are installed in this plane in front of the main door, at the emergency exit doors and at the forward crew's door. These chutes were installed so that passengers may quickly abandon the ship by sliding in case of an emergency landing. The crew has been adequately trained to use these chutes and their instructions should be followed without hesitancy.

IMPRESO EN MEXICO
PRINTED IN MEXICO

DAN-AIR SERVICES LTD.

SAFETY ON BOARD
PLEASE READ CAREFULLY (not to be taken away)

INTRODUCTION
In accordance with the regulations of the Board of Trade the following information is given for passengers in the event of an emergency.

SEAT BELTS
A seat belt is provided for each passenger seat and you are asked to note the method of quick release. The seat belt must always be fastened for take-off and landing and at any time when instructed by a crew member or when cabin sign is illuminated. When the illuminated sign "Fasten Seat Belts" is off you may unfasten your seat belt.

SMOKING
Smoking is not allowed during take-off or landing or when the illuminated signs read "No Smoking", not at any time in the toilets. Ash trays are provided in the arms of the chairs. On leaving the aircraft do NOT smoke until you are inside the Terminal Building.

EMERGENCY EXITS
You are asked to note the position of the windows and Exits which are marked with the words "Emergency Exit". The method of opening is clearly marked on each exit. Do not touch unless instructed by a crew member.

LIFE JACKETS
A life jacket is provided for each passenger and is stowed under your seat or in the seat pocket in front of you; read the simple instructions for its use, as shown in the illustration below.

In the case of a child, the life jacket must be partially inflated and fitted over the child's head. The tapes should be passed round the body, crossed at the back and then around the jacket at a position just below the waist. Tie off in a double knot at the back of the child.

BABIES FLOATING COTS
These are provided especially for the use of infants. Should they be required, the crew will give instructions for their use.

DINGHIES
Rubber dinghies are carried in accordance with regulations. If required, instructions will be given by a crew member.

RADIO INTERFERENCE
Due to the possibility of interference with the aircraft radio and navigation aids, operation of portable radios, tape recorders or other electronic equipment is not permitted at any time in the aircraft.

ESCAPE CHUTE
An escape chute is carried enabling exit from doors some height from the ground. If required, instructions will be given by a crew member.

EMERGENCY LANDING INSTRUCTIONS
In the event of an emergency landing you will be advised by the crew of the emergency and in this event you are asked to keep calm and follow their instructions.

The crew will advise you to:—

1. Loosen neckwear, put on any warm clothing, remove glasses, dentures, high-heeled shoes and empty pockets of any sharp objects.
2. Extinguish cigarettes and do NOT use lighters or matches.
3. Note position of nearest emergency exit.
4. Adjust the seat to the upright position and fasten your seat belt.
5. On hearing whistle blast it will mean "Brace for Landing" and this should be done as follows:
   (a) Forward-facing seats: sit straight in centre of chair, feet on floor slightly apart, cushion head on folded arms on lap.
   (b) Backward-facing seats: sit straight in centre of chair, head braced well back, hands gripping back of seat by head.
6. Be prepared for more than one impact.
7. When the aircraft has come to rest the crew will instruct you how and where to leave the aircraft. Their instructions should be followed implicitly.

1 Remove jacket from valise

2 Pass over head

3 Tie tapes round waist

4 Inflate by pulling red toggle

5 Re-inflate or top-up, using mouthpiece. To increase pressure, blow through the mouth valve. Reduce pressure by depressing the spigot in the valve mouth.

6 Illuminate light by pulling tab and removing cord. Pull cord till completely detached.

ADULTS MUST NOT INFLATE LIFE JACKET UNTIL AFTER LEAVING THE AIRCRAFT

Dan-Air Services—COMET FLEET (COMET 4C.)

YOUR SAFETY

is our first consideration and every possible precaution is taken to ensure it. These instructions are for your guidance should an emergency occur.

LIFEJACKETS

Put on lifejacket when instructed by crew but do not inflate jacket in cabin
Pull the lifejacket over the head—pass the tapes round the body, crossing them at the back and tying them securely in a double knot at the side of the body.

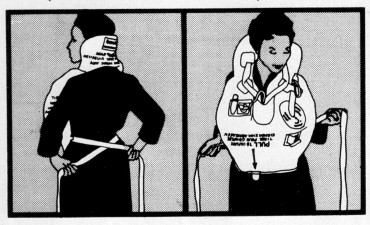

LIFEJACKETS FOR CHILDREN

For small children it is advisable to inflate the lifejacket before putting it on, otherwise the sound of inflation may frighten the child. It may be necessary partially to deflate the lifejacket to get it over the child's head. To fit, care should be taken to cross the tapes around the back **above the hips,** then return them to the front, crossing them over the top of the inflated buoyancy chamber and tying the ends across the child's back.

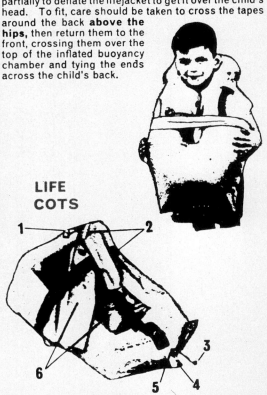

LIFE COTS

OXYGEN EQUIPMENT

All aircraft have pressurized cabins and in all aircraft oxygen is available for medical requirements. In Comet aircraft, should the cabin pressure have to be reduced, oxygen would automatically be made available to each passenger. Simple cup-shaped masks would drop out of overhead stowages but must be pulled down fully in order to turn on the oxygen, before being placed over the nose and mouth. **Cigarettes must be extinguished.**

Specially designed Life Cots are available on all our aircraft to ensure the safety of babies and children who are too small to be accommodated by the standard lifejacket. These cots will float safely and the partially transparent hood together with the insulated floor will give protection under all weather conditions. **To inflate and prepare for use:** (a) Remove cot from container. (b) Inflate by pulling red toggle smartly. (c) Wrap the child in a blanket and lay it on its side in the lifecot, fixing the straps diagonally. (d) Erect hood. **Note:** Do not erect hood until about to leave the aircraft.
1. Automatic light. 2. Carrying strap and line. 3. Inflation toggle. Pull to inflate. 4. Mouth inflation tube. 5. Deflating key. 6. Hood and window.

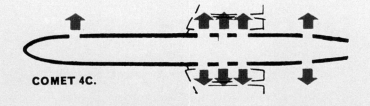

COMET 4C.

LEAVING THE AIRCRAFT IN THE EVENT OF AN EMERGENCY LANDING

introducing
Little Hassan . . .
with some essential
information which
you are asked
to study

SUDAN AIRWAYS

EMERGENCY EXITS

All Sudan Airways aircraft have ample emergency exits situated as follows:

The method of opening is marked on each exit but do not attempt to use these except on the crew's instructions.

COMET 4C

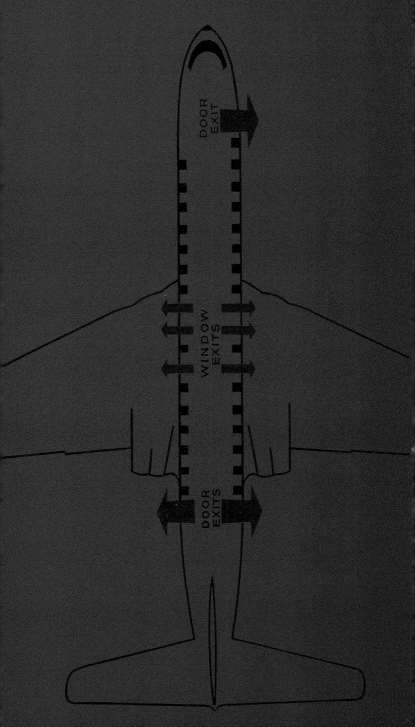

Page 61. United Arab Airlines, DH Comet. This card is from the late 1960s, prior to United Arab becoming Egyptair.

Page 63. BEA, Comet. This is one of several versions of the Comet safety card used by BEA during the aircraft's long operational period with the airline. This particular version was issued in the very late 1960s to replace the generic safety instructions placed in the airline's in-flight magazine.

Page 65. Mexicana, Comet. This is an extremely rare safety card, used in the late 1960s by North America's only Comet operator. Canadian Pacific and Pan Am had both ordered Comets but Pan Am's order was cancelled following the grounding of the Comet I, and Canadian Pacific's Comet crashed in India during its delivery flight.

Page 67. Dan-Air, Comet 4C. This is the last issue of Dan-Air's Comet card, used until the aircraft ceased operation in the late 1970s. Like many U.K. operators, Dan-Air placed their safety instructions in the in-flight magazine until the late 1960s/early 1970s when individual "cards" were issued for each aircraft type. For a very short period, Dan-Air experimented with safety instructions on placards affixed to the back of each seatback table. This system was later totally abandoned in favour of printed cards.

Page 69. Sudan Airways, Comet 4C, "Little Hassan". This card is probably from the early 1960s. An identical format was used on the airline's Viscount safety cards.

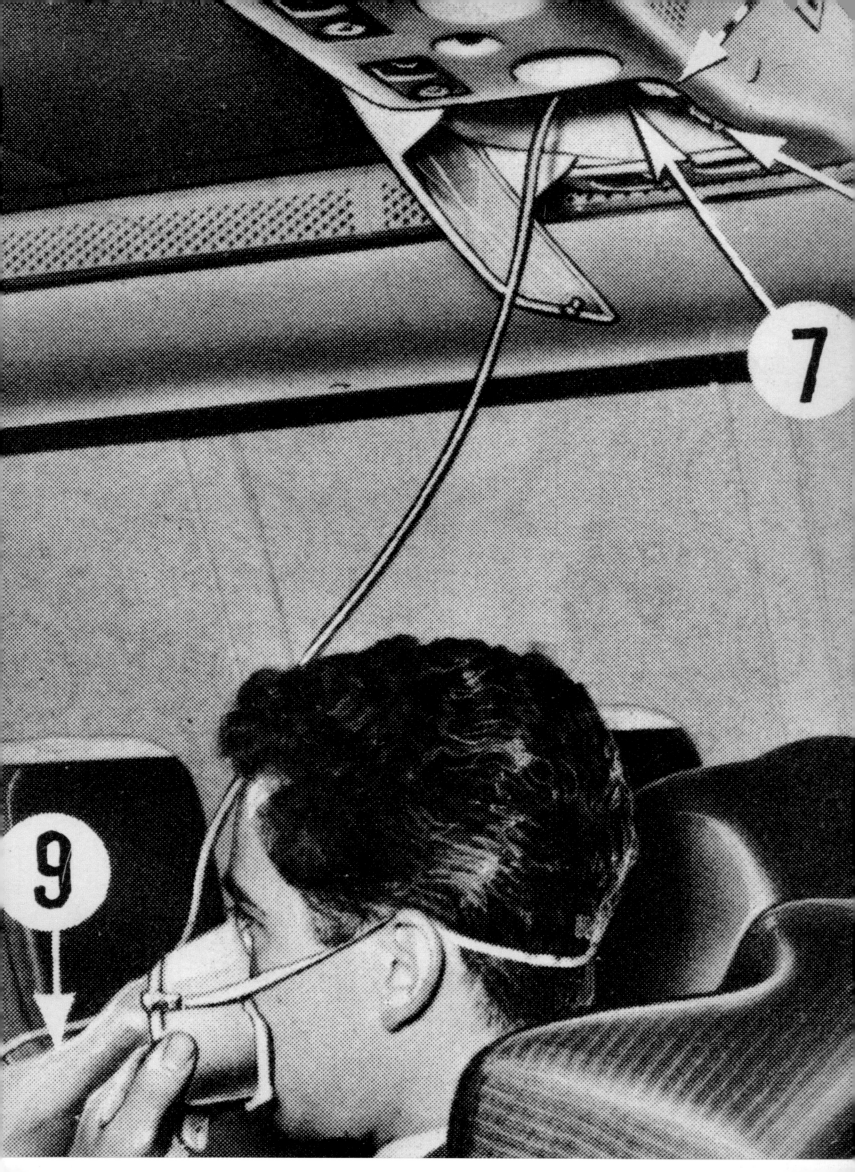

The Dash 80 prototype led to a revolution in air transportation. Although it never entered commercial service itself, it gave birth to the 707 series of jetliners. Much larger, faster and smoother than the propeller airplanes it was replacing, it quickly changed the face of international travel.

The first commercial 707s, labelled the 707-120 series, had a larger cabin than the prototype and other improvements. Powered by early Pratt & Whitney turbojet engines, these initial 707s had range capability that was barely sufficient for crossing the Atlantic Ocean. A number of variants were developed for special use, including shorter-bodied airplanes and the 720 series, which was lighter and faster with better runway performance, designed for shorter-distance flights.

Boeing quickly developed the larger 707-320 Intercontinental series, with a longer fuselage, larger wings and higher-powered engines. With these modifications, which allowed an increased fuel capacity from 56,781 litres (15,000 gallons) to over 87,064 litres (23,000 gallons), the 707 lived up to its name with a truly intercontinental range of over 6,437 km (4,000 miles), and could carry 141 passengers in a mixed-class seating configuration.

When the 707 production line was closed at the end of May 1991, Boeing had sold 1,010 aircraft of all types. Not bad for an aircraft designed in the early 1950s.

EMERGENCY INSTRUCTIONS

PAN AM

- MESURES DE SECURITE
- ANWEISUNGEN FÜR DEN NOTFALL
- ISTRUZIONI DI EMERGENZA
- INSTRUCCIONES DE EMERGENCIA
- INSTRUÇÕES PARA EMERGENCIA
- 處理緊急事故指導
- 非常の場合の心得

PAN AMERICAN
WORLD'S MOST EXPERIENCED AIRLINE

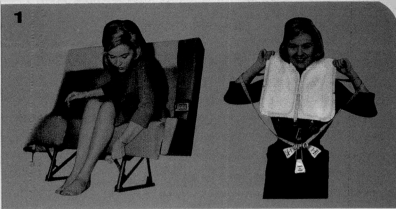

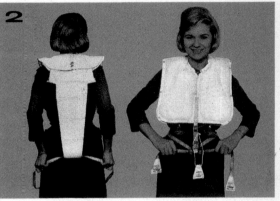

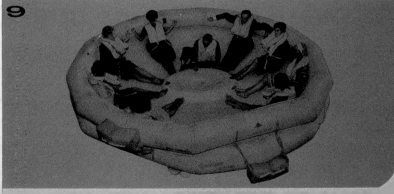

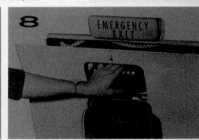

AWAITING RESCUE

AWAITING RESCUE

All Pan Am flights are guarded constantly by the Company's Flight Control organization. In addition, the International Civil Aviation Organization provides the means for search and rescue in every corner of the globe. Should an emergency occur these vast facilities are set in motion at once, enlisting all available surface and air transport, both civil and military.

ATTENTE DES SECOURS

Tous les vols de la Pan American sont constamment surveillés par les services de contrôle de la Compagnie. De plus, l'Organisation Internationale de l'Aviation Civile possède des moyens de recherche et de secours dans toutes les parties du globe. En cas d'urgence, tous ces moyens sont immédiatement mis en oeuvre, y compris tous les transports maritimes et aériens disponibles, aussi bien civils que militaires.

BERGUNG

Alle Pan Am Flüge werden ständig durch das Flugkontrollsystem der Gesellschaft überwacht. Darüber hinaus ermöglicht die Internationale Zivile Luftfahrt Organisation (ICAO) Suche und Rettung in allen Teilen der Erde. Sollte eine Notlage entstehen, dann treten diese weltweiten Rettungs—Möglichkeiten sofort in Aktion und ziehen dabei alle verfügbaren Land-, See- und Luftfahrzeuge, gleich ob ziviler oder militärischer Art, zur Hilfeleistung heran.

IN ATTESA DEI SOCCORSI

Tutti i voli della Pan American sono ininterottamente seguiti dall'organizzazione "Controllo Voli" a cura della compagnia stessa. Inoltre l'organizzazione internazionale dell'Aviazione Civile, ICAO, mantiene un servizio costante di vigilanza e di ricerca in ogni angolo del globo. In caso di emergenza, tutti questi dispositivi entrano in azione mentre ad essi si affianca qualsiasi altro mezzo di trasporto aereo o di superficie disponibile, sia civile che militare.

AGUARDANDO SOCORROS

Todos os aviões da Pan Am são constantemente acompanhados pelos vários Serviços de Controle da Companhia. A Organização de Aviação Civil fornece os meios para pesquisa e salvamento em todos os pontos do globo. Se se verificar um caso de emergência, estas facilidades serão imediatamente postas em acção, utilizando-se todo o género de transportes aéreos e terrestres, tanto civis como militares.

RESCATE

La organización de control de vuelos de la Pan American sigue constantemente el progreso de todos los vuelos de la compañía. Además, la Organización Internacional de Aviación Civil cuenta con medios de busqueda y salvamento en todas partes del mundo. Si llegara a presentarse una emergencia, todos sus servicios se pondrán inmediatamente en acción, utilizando todos los medios disponibles de transporte terrestre, marítimo o aéreo, tanto civil como militar.

等待援救

所有泛美航機，均與公司方面之飛行管制部作經常連絡。此外，國際民航協會有搜尋及救援設備，遍達世界任何角落。遇有緊急事件時，此龐大之救援組織，將能立即採取行動，民用及軍用之海陸空運輸單位，均儘可能應召協助援救。

救助隊の待機

パン・アメリカン航空のすべての飛行機は、会社の航空指令組織により常に監視されているのみならず、国際民間航空協会においても世界のすみずみまで探索及び救難活動ができるように万全を期しております。したがって、万一不慮の事故が発生した場合でも、全機能を動員して、対処いたします。付近航行中の軍及び民間の船舶ならびに飛行機をも即時に動員可能ですから、安心してご旅行を楽しんでいただけます。

PAN AMERICAN
WORLD'S MOST EXPERIENCED AIRLINE

SEAT BELTS

Experienced air travelers normally wear their seat belts fastened while seated even during periods when not required. This is recommended as an added convenience and precaution.

Normalement, les voyageurs aériens expérimentés maintiennent attaché leur ceinture de sécurité pendant qu'ils sont assis, même durant le temps de vol lorsque ceci n'est pas requis. Cette pratique est recommandée pour la convenance et comme une précaution supplémentaire.

Erfahrene Flugreisende sichern im allgemeinen ihren Gurt auch, wenn es nicht vorgeschrieben wird. Wir empfehlen dies als zusätzliche Bequemlichkeit und Vorsorge.

Esperti viaggiatori tengono di solito la cintura allacciata quando sono seduti anche nei momenti in cui non è richiesto. Questo è raccomandabile come ulteriore precauzione e comodità.

Normalmente, os passageiros aéreos experimentados mantêm assegurado seu cinto de segurança quando estão assentados, mesmo durante os períodos de vôo quando esta precaução não é exigida. Esta prática é recommendado como uma conveniência e uma precaução adicional.

Normalmente, los pasajeros aéros experimentados mantienen asegurado su cinturón de seguridad mientras que están sentados, incluso durante los períodos de vuelo cuando esta precaución no se exige. Se recomienda hacer ésto como una conveniencia y una precaución adicional.

有經驗的旅客，即使在飛行中不需要的時候，也往往將安全帶繫上。為方便及增加安全起見，我們認為這樣做法值得介紹。

旅なれた空の旅行客は、普通、特別その必要のない時でも座席ベルトをしめています。これは万一の非常事態に対する備えであり、皆さまも常時安全ベルトを使用されることをおすすめします。

PRINTED IN U.S.A.   9243-7399

BOEING
Jet INTERCONTINENTAL

Lieber Fluggast!

Jederzeit werden Sie an Bord der komfortablen Boeing Jet Intercontinental das Gefühl haben, daß LUFTHANSA alles für das Wohlbefinden ihrer Gäste tut. Sollte dennoch einmal ein nicht vorherzusehender Notfall eintreten, so bitten wir Sie, sich genau nach den folgenden Sicherheitsinstruktionen zu richten, die den Bestimmungen der internationalen Luftfahrtbehörde entsprechen.

Falls wirklich das Verlassen des Flugzeuges erforderlich sein sollte, so stehen genügend Schlauchboote zur Verfügung — sie bieten jeweils 26 Passagieren Platz. Unsere bestens geschulten Besatzungsmitglieder bringen die Boote zu Wasser und sorgen für Ihre sichere Unterbringung.

Mit einem starken Notsender im Boot kann die Rettungsaktion schnell eingeleitet werden. Ein ständig überwachtes Flugkontrollsystem ermöglicht Suche und Rettung in allen Teilen der Welt. Zivile und militärische Land-, See- und Luftfahrzeuge stehen ständig bereit, wirksame Hilfe zu leisten.

Dear Passenger,

On board our comfortable Boeing Jet Intercontinental you will always have the feeling that LUFTHANSA does everything for its passengers to make them feel at ease. Should an emergency case ever occur, we kindly ask you to comply with the following safety instructions established in accordance with the International Safety Regulations for Aviation.

In case you have to leave the aircraft sufficient liferafts are aboard for everyone, each with room for 26 persons. Our well trained crew will launch the rafts and care for your accommodation.

The equipment of the raft includes a powerful radio transmitter to facilitate quick rescue. A constantly alert organisation provides search and rescue in every part of the world. Civil and military land-, sea- and air rescue facilities are permanently available for this purpose.

A nos aimables passagers!

A bord du confortable Boeing Jet Intercontinental vous aurez toujours l'impression que la LUFTHANSA fait tout ce qui se trouve en son pouvoir pour que vous vous sentiez bien à l'aise. Si toutefois un cas exceptionnel de danger surgit, nous vous prions de suivre attentivement les mesures de sécurité suivantes, imposées par les prescriptions internationales.

En cas d'amerrissage forcé, il y a suffisamment de canots de sauvetage pour tout le monde — chacun d'eux ayant place pour 26 passagers. Les membres de l'équipage, parfaitement entraînés, mettront les canots à l'eau et s'occuperont de votre embarquement. A bord de chaque canot se trouve un émetteur- récepteur qui accélérera votre sauvetage. Un service de contrôle aérien constamment surveillé possède des moyens de recherche et de secours dans toutes les parties du globe. Des moyens de transport terrestres, maritimes et aériens aussi bien civils que militaires — sont constamment à la disposition pour accomplir une action sauvetage efficace.

LUFTHANSA

4

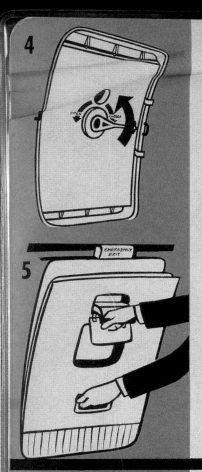

Notausgänge

Die hierfür vorgesehenen Tür- und Fensterausgänge sind deutlich gekennzeichnet. An jedem Ende der Hauptkabine befinden sich 2 Ausgänge — links der Hauptausgang und gegenüber die Küchenladetür (Bild 4) — die Fensterausgänge liegen in der Mitte der Kabine und führen auf die Tragflächen (Bild 5).
Die Türen werden vom Begleitpersonal geöffnet, zum Öffnen der Fenster ist am darüber befindlichen Griff zu ziehen.
Für den Halt auf der Tragfläche werden Taue gespannt.

Emergency Exits

Door and window exits are clearly marked. There are two exits at each end of the passenger compartment, the main exit at the left side and opposite the galley door (illustration No. 4) — the window exits in the middle of the cabin leading onto the wings (illustr. No. 5).
The doors will be opened by the crew. In order to open the window pull handle above the window.
For assistance in leaving aircraft a rope will be attached from top of exit to top of wing.

5

Sorties de secours

Les portes et les hublots servant de sorties de secours sont clairement indiqués comme tels. A chaque extrémité de la cabine principale se trouvent deux sorties — à gauche l'entrée principale, et en face de celle-ci, donc du côté droit, la porte près des cuisines (croquis 4). Les hublots servant de sorties de secours sont situés au milieu de la cabine et donnent accès aux ailes (croquis 5). Le personnel de bord ouvrira les portes. Pour déverrouiller les hublots, tirez sur la poignée placée au-dessus.
Pour pouvoir vous maintenir en équilibre sur les ailes, les membres de l'équipage y tendront des cordes de secours.

6

Verlassen des Flugzeuges durch die Fenster

Nachdem das Flugzeug zum Stillstand gekommen ist — nicht vorher — schnallen Sie den Sitzgurt durch Anheben des Schloßdeckels los und warten die Anweisungen der Besatzung ab.
Müssen Sie das Flugzeug durch einen als Notausstieg gekennzeichnetes Tragflächenfenster verlassen, dann ist folgende Reihenfolge wichtig: Erst ein Bein, dann Kopf, Oberkörper und das andere Bein.

Leaving the aircraft through window exits

When the plane stops — not before — unfasten your seat belt and await instructions from the crew.
In case of debarking from aircraft through one of the emergency exit wing windows the following sequence is important: first one leg, then the head, the upper part of the body and the other leg.

Evacuation de l'avion par les hublots

Après l'immobilisation de l'avion — pas avant — débouclez votre ceinture de sécurité en soulevant le dispositif de fermeture et attendez les instructions que vous donneront les membres de l'équipage.
Si vous devez sortir par une sortie de secours située au-dessus d'une aile, il est indispensable pour une évacuation rapide de suivre le procédé suivant:
passez d'abord une jambe par le hublot, ensuite la tête, puis le reste du corps et enfin l'autre jambe.

7

Aufblasen der Schwimmweste

Nach Verlassen des Flugzeuges — nicht eher — ziehen Sie ruckartig die beiden Knöpfe nach unten, und die Weste bläst sich selbsttätig auf.
Die Weste kann auch mit dem Mundschlauch aufgeblasen werden.

How to inflate the life vest

When outside the aircraft — not before — inflate life vest by a sharp pull down on the two inflation knobs. The life vest may also be inflated by using the mouth tube.

Gonflage du gilet de sauvetage

Après avoir quitté l'avion — pas avant — tirez énergiquement les deux gonfleurs vers le bas, le gilet se gonflera automatiquement.
Vous pouvez aussi gonfler le gilet en soufflant dans l'embouchure.

Printed in Germany (West)
Wbg. 322 001 190/160/HL

8

Sauerstoffversorgung

Die Menge an mitgeführtem Sauerstoff reicht in Notfällen für alle Passagiere aus. Wenn erforderlich, kommt aus einem Fach über Ihrem Sitz automatisch eine Maske herab. Ziehen Sie die Maske zu sich heran und drücken Sie diese beim Atmen fest auf Mund und Nase.
Bei Entnahme von reinem Sauerstoff besteht erhöhte Brandgefahr, deshalb Vorsicht mit offener Flamme.

Oxygen supply

Oxygen is provided for all passengers. In an emergency the mask for breathing oxygen will automatically drop out of the overhead service unit. Pull it towards you and hold it firmly over both nose and mouth and breathe normally.
While taking oxygen DO NOT SMOKE.

Oxygène

La quantité d'oxygène emmagasinée à bord est suffisante pour tous les passagers.
En cas d'urgence, un masque à oxygène sort automatiquement d'un emplacement situé au-dessus de votre tête. Tirez-le vers vous et à chaque aspiration serrez-le contre le nez et la bouche.
Pendant la diffusion de l'oxygène il est strictement défendu de fumer.

9

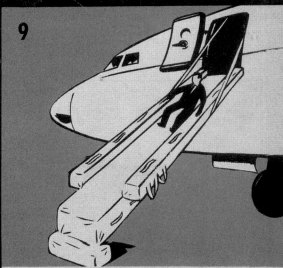

Notrutschen

An jedem der Ausgänge (Haupt- und Küchentüren) befindet sich zur schnellen Räumung der Maschine eine aufblasbare Rutsche.
Wenn diese von der Besatzung ausgebracht sind, springen Sie hinein und rutschen hinunter, ziehen Sie dabei nicht die Beine an.
Ältere Personen können vor dem Rutschen Sitzstellung einnehmen.

Emergency Chutes

For rapid evacuation a chute which can be inflated is installed at each exit (main doors and service doors). After the crew has placed the chute in position, jump and slide down. Do not pull up your legs. Elderly persons should slide down in a sitting position.

Plans inclinés

A chaque sortie (porte principale et portes pour le chargement des cuisines) se trouve une glissière pneumatique pour une évacuation rapide de l'avion.
Sitôt que ces glissières seront sorties et fixées par les membres de l'équipage, montez dessus et glissez vers le sol. Raidissez vos jambes de façon à ne pas culbuter en avant.
Il est permis aux personnes âgées de s'asseoir sur le plan incliné avant de se laisser glisser jusqu'en bas.

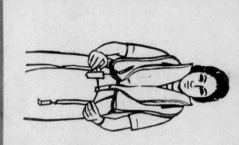

EMERGENCY INSTRUCTIONS

BOEING 720-B

THESE INSTRUCTIONS SHOULD BE READ CAREFULLY AND
FOLLOWED METICULOUSLY IN THE EVENT OF EMERGENCY

নিম্নলিখিত নিয়মাবলী সতর্কতার সঙ্গে পড়ুন এবং জরুরী অবস্থার সময় অত্যন্তবিচারে ভাবে চলুন

1

IF THE AIRCRAFT IS FORCED TO ALIGHT OVER WATER THE CAPTAIN WILL INSTRUCT YOU TO PUT ON YOUR LIFE JACKET

1. LIFE JACKET—You will find your life jacket in a pocket under your seat. It can be put on from either side. Hold it in front of you and pass it over your head.

2

2. Connect the waist straps to the hooks and tighten them by pulling the ends.

3

3. The life jacket inflates automatically by giving a sharp pull on two plastic knobs.

4

4. The life jacket can also be inflated by blowing air by mouth, through these tubes.

5

5. ESCAPE SLIDE-Door exits are equipped with special slides to aid escape to the ground. Obey instructions of the crew, who know how the slides should be used.

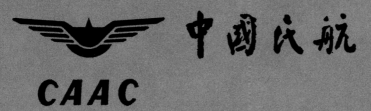

中國民航
CAAC

波 音 **707B**
BOEING

旅客安全须知

PASSENGER SAFETY INFORMATION

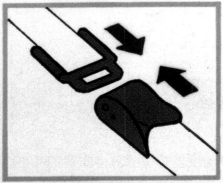

安全带
SEAT BELT

飞机起飞、降落和颠簸时，请系上安全带。

Please fasten your seat belt during take-off, landing and when turbulence occurs.

请勿吸烟
NO SMOKING

飞机起飞和降落时，请勿吸烟。

Please don't smoke during take-off and landing.

氧气口罩　OXYGEN MASK

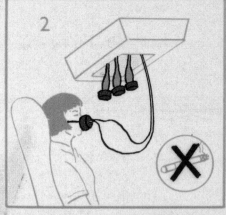

氧气口罩贮藏箱在您座椅的上方，当座舱高度达 4200 公尺时，口罩自动下垂，使用时将口罩拉下戴好，正常呼吸。

Oxygen masks are kept in the stowage above your seat. When the cabin reaches the altitude of 4200 metres, they will automatically drop from the stowage. When using it, just pull an oxygen mask down, wear it and breathe normally.

救生衣　LIFE JACKET

1.救生衣在您座椅下面口袋内，使用时取出套在颈上。
Your life jacket is in the bag under your seat. When using it, take it from the bag and pull it over your head.

2.把飘带由前向后系在腰间。
Tie the band round your waist.

3.往下拉阀门绳，救生衣就会充气。
Pull the valve string to inflate your life jacket.

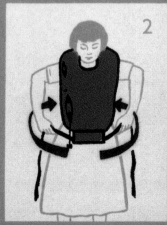

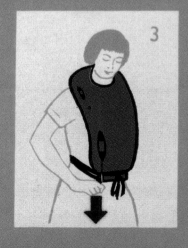

707 NIGERIA AIRWAYS
safety instructions

Oxygen

1 2 3

Your lifejacket
do not inflate inside the aircraft

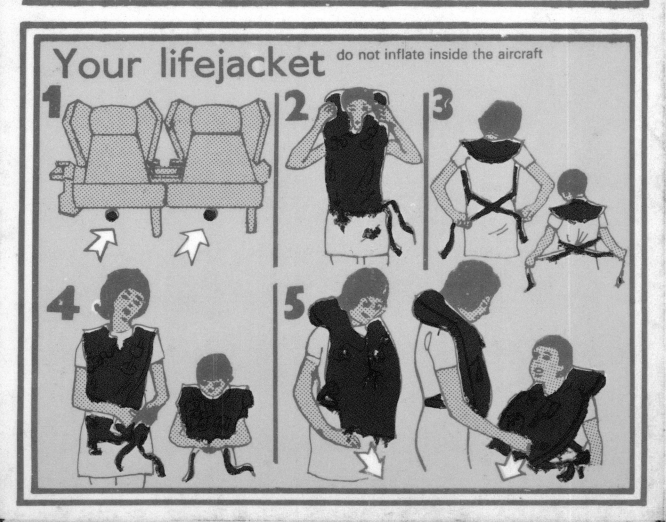

1 2 3

4 5

Emergency Exits

Doors

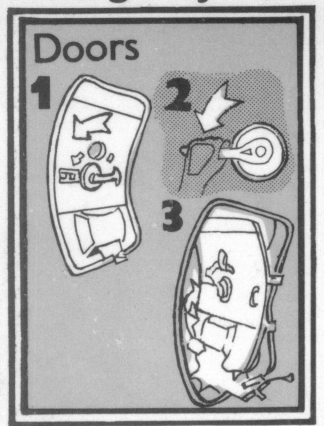

Windows

Escape routes

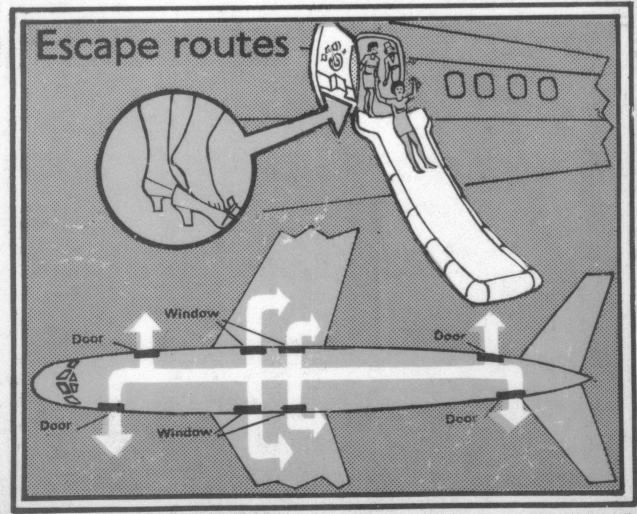

Printed by Nigeria Airways Press, Ikeja/021/4/78

Page 77. Pan Am, Boeing 707. This was the first Pan Am safety card for jet aircrafts, and also the first 707 card ever issued. It dates from 1958.

Page 79. Lufthansa, Boeing 707. This is the first Lufthansa jet card, dating from 1960.

Page 81. PIA, Boeing 720. This was the first PIA card for jet aircraft, and dates from the early 1960s. The non-inflatable, hand-held escape slides were replaced by inflatable ones in the mid-1960s.

Page 83. CAAC, Boeing 707B. This is the first CAAC 707 card. The airline took delivery of its first US-built aircraft in 1973.

Page 85. Nigeria Airways, Boeing 707. This card dates from the early 1970s.

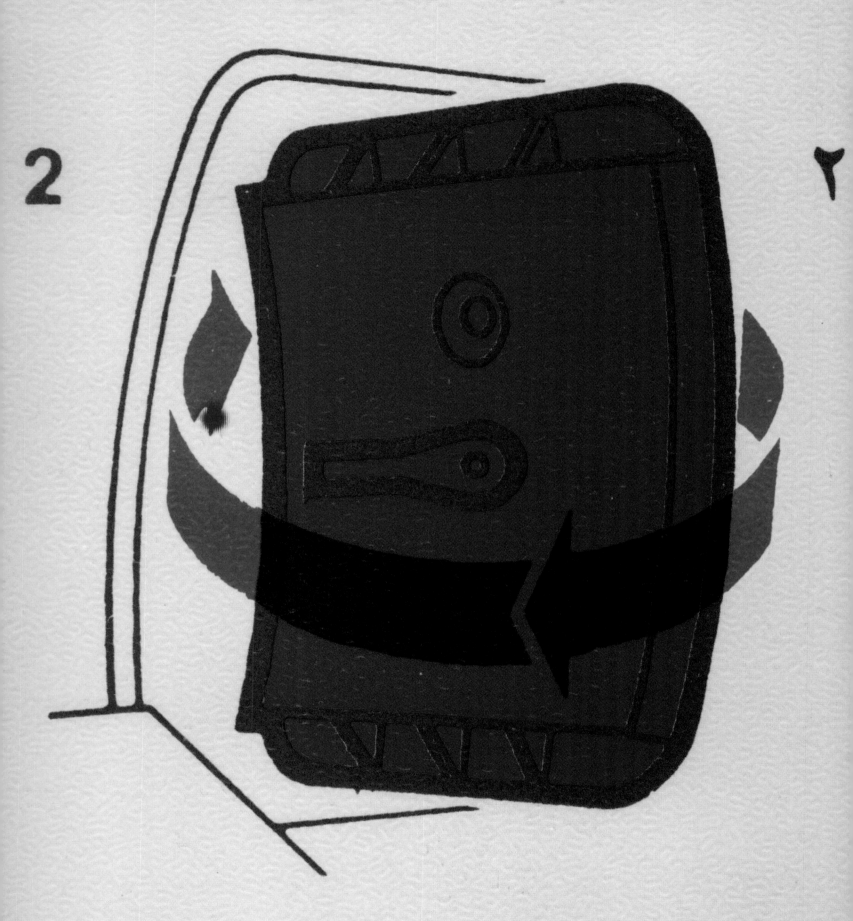

وَمِنْ ثَمَّ افتَح البَابَ
نَحوَ الخَارِجِ.

PASSENGERS DESCENDING OVER LEADING EDGE OF WING, BEING ASSISTED DOWN.

The Douglas DC-8

It was on Memorial Day in the U.S., 30 May 1958, that the Douglas DC-8 made its maiden flight. Although the Boeing 707 beat the DC-8 being taken into traffic one year earlier, the DC-8 was just as significant in terms of encouraging the airlines to take up jet aircraft. The DC-8 was somewhat bigger than the 707, and had a slightly better fuel range, which prompted Boeing to alter its airplane to match its competitor. Both of the models had their own "supporters". They were designed for the same type of use – long-distance routes – and a few airlines, Pan Am for instance, actually operated them both. In 1997, Boeing merged with McDonnell-Douglas, ending their fierce competition. The DC-8 and the 707 had long been out of production, although they are still in use all over the world. Over 40 years after the DC-8's maiden flight, 294 of the 556 models produced between 1958 and 1972 remain in service with 50 operators around the world, and are doing more than 270 scheduled passenger flights a day, to and from 140 cities in 58 countries.

The design of DC-8 safety cards is very similar to that of the Boeing 707. Both aircraft were very successful models, having served the world's airlines for years. The cards show a wide variety of aesthetic approaches, ranging from late-1950s optimism to modern-day graphics. The first JAL safety card was a DC-8 one. As with the 707, early DC-8 cards tend to be rather complicated, with later examples taking a more pedagogic line in their representation of safety routines.

The four-engine DC-8 set commercial transport world records for speed, altitude, distance and payload in its first decade. From its inception, it embodied advanced aerodynamic and structural concepts, as well as internal systems designed for maximum service reliability, operational convenience and passenger comfort. Four basic models were produced: the Series 10 through 50, in passenger, freighter and convertible freighter versions; and the Super 60 Series 61, 62 and 63, with freighter models of each. The last of 556 aircraft in the 707 series was delivered on 13 May 1972, marking the end of 15 years of production, at which time there were 48 operators in 28 nations.

Development of the Super 60 Series in 1965, with increased size, capacity and efficiency, demonstrated the capacity for growth in the DC-8 design. The Super 61 and 62 can carry up to 258 passengers. The Super 63, which combined the fuselage extension and payload capacity of the Super 61 with the long-range, aerodynamic and power plant improvements of the Super 62, carries a maximum capacity of 259 passengers 7,242 km (4,500 miles), or at lesser loads even greater distances. The DC-8 Super 63F/63CF is able to carry up to 52,617 kg (116,000 pounds) of freight. It held the title of the world's largest passenger aircraft until 1969, when the Boeing 747 "Jumbo Jet" was introduced.

The DC-8 Series 70 is a re-engined version of the popular Super 60 Series, substituting CFM56 engines for Pratt & Whitney ones. The result is an aircraft that retains the Super 60 operating weights, but with a longer range due to the newer, more fuel-efficient turbofans. The Series 70 was also able to meet the more stringent noise regulations that were implemented in the 1980s. All this has guaranteed the DC-8's place in the history of commercial air transport design.

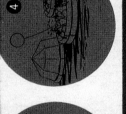

DC-8C

● LOCATION OF EXITS 緊急時の出口

Comment Mettre Votre Gilet de Sauvetage

① Vous trouverez des gilets de sauvetage sous chaque banc.

② Le gilet de sauvetage se met tout comme on revêt un gilet. Ensuite, prenez les agrafes des deux côtés et fixez les dans les yeux centrals ayant la forme d'un "D". Finalle ment, tirez les courroies de la taille qui serrent les courroies autour de votre taille.

③ Pour souffler le gilet, tirez les poignées de chaque coté. NE SOUFFLEZ PAS LE GILET QUAND VOUS ETES DANS L'AVION.

④ Cependant, si le gilet n'est pas gonflé suffisamment relâchez le couvercle (embouchure) et soufflez dedans. Resserrz le couvercle quand le gilet sera suffisamment gonflé. Si vous avez des enfants avec vous, demandez un appareil d'enfant à l'assistant de cabine.

救生衣的穿法

① 救生衣是垫在座位的下邊，穿法如下：

② 打開救生衣，像毛衣那樣由咽上穿進，把右邊的搭扣扣插在右邊的"D"字型環上，左邊的搭扣扣插在左邊的"D"字型環上，拉兩條的腰帶，適当地結好。

③ 只需用力向下拉左右拉亞手，救生衣就能充上空气而膨脹。但在飛机内绝不要充進空气。

④ 如救生衣未膨脹的不够，請打開嘴管口，吹進空气。吹气重複吏至救生用的救生衣。

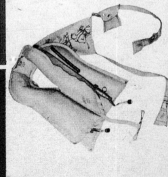

緊急時の心得　急救須知

EMERGENCY
INSTRUCTION

INSTRUCTION EN
CAS D'URGENCE

INSTRUCCIONES DE
EMERGENCIA

緊急情況須知

本飛機不論在安全性方面或舒適性方面都是優秀的客機。但是，為了準備在萬一發生緊急情況時，特備有救生衣，救急備品及其他必要的裝備。更因為處理緊急情況均受有充分的訓練，所以在緊急情況發生時務請聽從服務員的指示，沉着地行動。如下各項是緊急情況時必要的知識，請仔細閱読。

落 水 時

緊急落水時，請採取如下行動。

① 請鬆開領帶、鈕頭、脫靴，由身體和衣服上拿掉如眼鏡、自來水筆和其他尖類的東西，穿着請穿上救生衣。

② 請把椅子靠背直立起來，在腰部墊上毛氈，上繫好子上的帶，為準備落水，請採取如下圖的姿勢，直到飛機完全停止為止，要採取這樣姿勢不變。

③ 落水後，不要着慌，聽從服務員的指示，由機艙門或太平門，有秩序的出到平地救生艇再放進空氣，否則會阻礙救生艇上。

④ 坐到救生艇到出後，請沉着地等待救護隊來臨，在救生艇上備有無線電…藥品。

En Cas D'urgence…

L'avion à réaction DC-8C possède les plus récents développements en confort et en sûreté. Il est pourvu de gilets de sauvetage et de tous les équipements nécessaires pour faire face à tous les cas d'urgence.

Les équipes de "Japan Air Lines" sont entraînées pour envisager n'importe quel cas d'urgence et vous donneront des instructions si quelque chose d'anormal survenait. S'il arrivait quelque chose, nous vous prions de demeurer calme et de suivre leurs instructions.

Pour votre commodité, nous vous offrons les instructions suivantes:

Descente Inévitable dans L'eau:

Si c'était nécessaire d'amérir, suivez les instructions suivantes:

① Détachez cravate et collet. Enlevez vos chaussures et vos lunettes. Sortez votre stylo ou autres objets pointus de vos poches. Mettez votre gilet de sauvetage.

② Placez le siège dans la position verticale. Mettez une couverture pliée ou un oreiller et attachez la ceinture de votre siège. Asseyez-vous de la manière indiquée dans la photo ci-dessous et restez à votre siège dans cette position jusqu'à ce que l'avion arrête et soit stable dans l'eau.

③ Quand l'avion arrête, sortez par la porte d'urgence la plus près de vous. Soyez calme quand vous embarquez sur le radeau. RAPPELEZ-VOUS QUE VOUS NE DEVEZ PAS SOUFFLER VOTRE APPAREIL DE SAUVETAGE AVANT DE SORTIR DE L'AVION.

④ Quand vous serez sur le radeau, restez calme jusqu'à ce que le bateau ou l'avion de sauvetage arrive. Tous les radeaux sont pourvus de transmetteurs radiophoniques, vus de transmetteurs radiophoniques, d'appel, courge, nourriture, des médicaments, etc., afin que vous ayez les premiers secours jusqu'à l'arrivée des sauveteurs.

PHOTOS NORMAND

Gilet de sauvetage Life belt jacket

Votre gilet de sauvetage (fig. 1) est déposé à proximité immédiate de votre siège : sa place exacte vous est indiquée par le personnel de bord. Passer le gilet par dessus la tête (fig. 2). Mettre les cordons autour de la taille et les fixer devant (fig. 3). Serrer la ceinture en tirant sur les cordons. Pour gonfler le gilet, tirez fortement sur les deux cordonnets (pendant à la partie inférieure) (fig. 4) ou éventuellement, utilisez les deux valves de gonflage à bouche.
Ne gonflez pas votre gilet avant d'en avoir reçu l'ordre.

Your life belt (fig. 1) is placed within easy reach of your seat ; you have been shown exactly where it is by a member of the crew. Slip on life belt over your head (fig. 2). Put laces around your waist (fig. 3). Pull on laces to tie the jacket on the front of you. To inflate the safety belt, pull sharply on the two little cords which hang from the lower portion (fig. 4), or should the occasion arise, use the two valves provided for inflating by the mouth. Do not inflate your life belt before given the order.

Position à prendre en cas d'atterrissage forcé
Position to take up in case of a forced landing

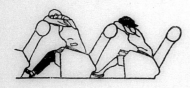

Sauf indications contraires des membres de l'équipage, inclinez complètement votre siège vers l'arrière, asseyez-vous bien au fond de votre fauteuil ; bouclez votre ceinture de siège en vous assurant qu'elle est bien ajustée et convenablement serrée. Les jambes arc-boutées, prenez appui avec les pieds contre le bâti du siège précédant le vôtre. Penchez-vous en avant ; appuyez votre front sur vos avant-bras croisés sur le dossier du siège situé devant vous (ou, suivant le cas, sur la table).

Unless told to do otherwise by a member of the crew, let your seat back as far as possible ; get well down in the depth of your chair ; fasten your seat belt, making sure that it is well adjusted and comfortably tightened. With legs apart, firmly press with your feet against the framework of the chair in front of you. Lean forward, rest your forehead against your forearm crossed on the back of the seat (or table, as the case may be) in front of you.

Si vous êtes assis face à l'arrière de la cabine, ajustez soigneusement votre ceinture de siège, calez-vous bien dans votre fauteuil, appuyez la tête sur le dossier de votre siège et prenez solidement appui sur les accoudoirs.

If you are sitting facing the rear of the cabin, adjust your safety belt carefully, wedge yourself well into your armchair lean your head against the back of the seat and grip the arm rest firmly.

Si vous occupez la première rangée de fauteuils, asseyez-vous sur le plancher, le dos appuyé contre la cloison avant, pliez les genoux, joignez fermement les mains sur la nuque et appuyez la tête contre la cloison.

If you are sitting in the first row of seats, sit on the floor with your back pressed against the foreward bulkhead, bend your knees, clasp your hands firmly behind the nape of your neck and press your head against the bulkhead.

Si la place entre la première rangée de fauteuils et la cloison est insuffisante pour adopter la position ci-dessus, posez les jambes sur votre siège en ayant soin de caler votre dos avec votre oreiller ou votre couverture.

If there is not enough room between the first row of seats and the bulkhead to take up the position described above, place your legs on your seat taking care to wedge your back with a cushion or rug.

En cas d'atterrissage ou d'amerrissage forcé, conformez-vous aux instructions suivantes :

— Desserrez cravate, col et tout vêtement entourant le cou.

— Enlevez vos lunettes.

— Otez de vos poches tous les objets pointus.

— En cas d'amerrissage seulement, retirez vos chaussures si elles ont des talons hauts ou des semelles cloutées et mettez vos vêtements les plus chauds.

In the event of a forced descent either on land or on the water, follow these instructions:

— Loosen you tie, collar and any other garment round the neck.

— Take off your spectacles.

— Empty your pockets of any sharp pointed instruments.

— In the event of a descent on the water only, take off your shoes if they have high heels or hobnailed soles and put on your warmest clothes.

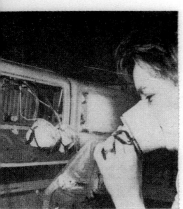

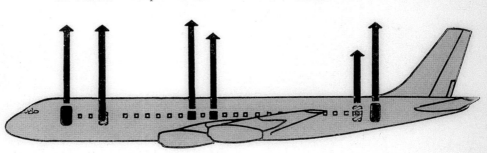

MASQUES A OXYGÈNE
Si la boîte à masques s'ouvre, prendre rapidement un masque et l'appliquer sur le visage.

OXYGEN MASKS
Should the compartment containing the oxygen mask open, pick up the mask quickly and apply it to the face.

ISSUES DE SECOURS
Fig. 1 - Pour ouvrir de l'intérieur tirer fort sur la poignée rouge.
Fig. 2 - Pour ouvrir de l'extérieur, pousser fort sur la plaque rouge.

EMERGENCY EXIT
Fig. 1 - To open from the inside, pull strongly on the red handle.
Fig. 2 - To open from the outside, push strongly on the red plaque.

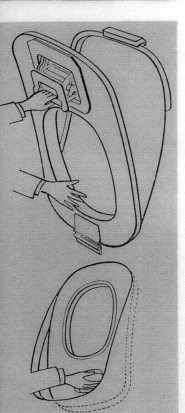

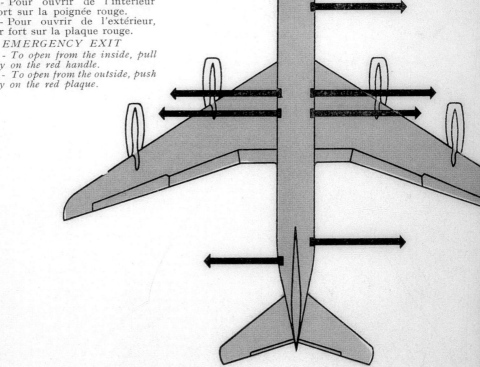

L'appareil est muni d'issues de secours qui vous sont indiquées par le personnel de bord. Ne quittez pas votre place avant l'immobilisation complète de l'avion. En cas d'évacuation, suivez en ordre et dans le calme les instructions données par le Commandant de bord et l'équipage qui mettront en œuvre le matériel collectif de secours.

The aircraft is provided with emergency exits indicated to your by the crew. Do not leave your seat before the aircraft has come completely to a stop. In the event of evacuating the aircraft, follow calmly and in an orderly manner the orders of the Captain and Crew who will put all the safety equipment into action.

IMP. BLONDIAUX - RK 3900

ONA

SUPER DC-8

OVERSEAS NATIONAL AIRWAYS

SAFETY PROCEDURES

You are flying aboard a DC-8-63F, with a Captain and Crew who are thoroughly trained and experienced. There is little likelihood we will encounter a situation requiring emergency preparations but it is a good practice to be acquainted with the safety features we have provided for you on this airplane.

PLEASE DO NOT TAKE THIS CARD FROM THE AIRCRAFT

JETESCAPE DOOR AUTOMATIC SLIDE OPERATION

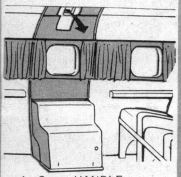

1. Grasp HANDLE — pull FIRMLY INWARD and DOWN
2. RELEASE handle as door falls outward

WINDOW EXIT OPERATION

1. Pull handle inward
2. Grasp bottom and top of window
3. Lift window in

BRACING POSITION

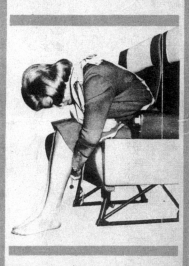

DOOR OPERATION

1. Lift handle fully
2. As hinged side moves in—push other side out
3. Latch open

INFLATABLE EVACUATION SLIDE (At all entry, galley and jetescape doors.)

SEAT BELTS

Move around as much as you like in the Cabin while the seat belt sign is off. We suggest, however, that you keep your seat belt loosely fastened while in your seats. Of course, seat belts must be fastened any time the seat belt sign is on.

NO SMOKING

When the "NO SMOKING" sign is off, you may smoke cigarettes while seated anywhere in the Cabin. Whenever the "NO SMOKING" sign comes on, however, all smokes are to be extinguished.

PLEASE SEE REVERSE SIDE ▶

OXYGEN SYSTEM

To make your flight comfortable and speedy, modern Jets such as this one operate at very high altitudes. In the unlikely event that cabin pressure should be lost, the thin air at these levels would require that you breathe supplemental oxygen. Should the need arise, a mask compartment over your seat would open automatically, and oxygen would flow to the masks if the reduction in cabin pressure is enough to make it necessary. If the compartment should open—

1. Pull nearest mask to your face and press open side over nose and mouth.
2. Breathe normally.
3. Adjust headband.
4. Wear mask until advised by Crew to remove it.

LIFE PRESERVERS

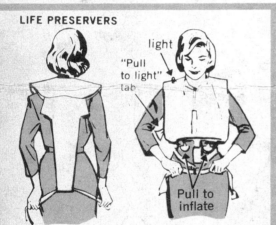

light

"Pull to light" tab

Pull to inflate

We are equipped with sufficient life preservers and life rafts to provide for all passengers and crew. The life preservers are under each seat and Raft locations are indicated on the EXIT diagram. To prepare for a landing on water you;

1. Follow instructions of Crew.
2. Put Life Preserver on (see diagram).
   Note: Children bring straps between legs and then engage.
3. Raise seat back to upright position.
4. Assume bracing position (see diagram).
5. After plane stops completely, unfasten Seat belt. Follow instructions of Crew.
6. After leaving plane, inflate Life Preserver.
7. Board raft, as directed by Crew.

This Airplane is in constant contact with Flight Control Center and rescue operations would be initiated immediately upon notification of an imminent water landing.

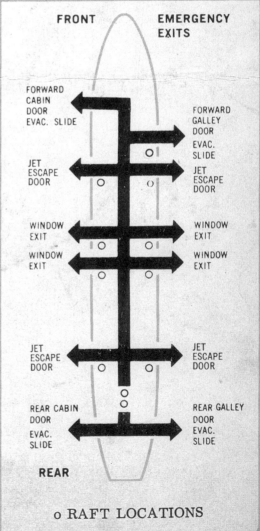

FRONT   EMERGENCY EXITS

FORWARD CABIN DOOR EVAC. SLIDE

FORWARD GALLEY DOOR EVAC. SLIDE

JET ESCAPE DOOR

JET ESCAPE DOOR

WINDOW EXIT

WINDOW EXIT

WINDOW EXIT

WINDOW EXIT

JET ESCAPE DOOR

JET ESCAPE DOOR

REAR CABIN DOOR EVAC. SLIDE

REAR GALLEY DOOR EVAC. SLIDE

REAR

o RAFT LOCATIONS

SAS safety on board...

DC-8 — automatic oxygen system

These aircraft fly at very high altitude. Should a sudden drop in the cabin pressure occur, oxygen will be needed immediately.
In the event of such a pressure drop a flap in the seat-back in front of you, or in a panel above you, will automatically open, presenting masks for oxygen breathing. A cord connects each mask with its valve. Grip the yellow mask firmly and pull it toward you, this will automatically open the oxygen valve. Place the mask over your nose and mouth. Fasten the mask with the headband. Breathe normally. Continue to use the mask until you are advised that you can remove it. Extra masks are available for infants. On Caravelle aircraft portable oxygen equipment will be provided by the cabin crew.

DC-8 — automatisk surstoff — (ilt) (syrgas) anlegg

Da disse flyene flyr på store høyder, må det automatiske surstoffanlegg øyeblikkelig tas i bruk ved en hastig trykkforandring i kabinen.
I en slik situasjon vil en klaff i stolryggen foran eller i taket ovenfor Dem automatisk åpnes og De finner en surstoffmaske. Et snøre forbinder masken med en ventil. Far den gule masken til ansiktet hvorved surstoffsventilen automatisk åpnes. Trykk den gule masken over nese og munn og fest den bakom hodet med gummistrikken. Pust (trekk været) (andas) normalt. Fortsett å bruke masken til annen beskjed blir gitt. For barn finnes det ekstramasker. I Caravelle-flyene vil portabelt surstoffutstyr bli delt ut av kabinpersonalet.

DC-8 — Système automatique d'inhalateurs d'oxygène

En raison des hautes altitudes auxquelles volent ces appareils, il est nécessaire de se servir au plus vite des inhalateurs d'oxygène si un changement soudain de pression intervient dans la cabine.
Si ce changement se produit, un battant ménagé dans le dossier du fauteuil placé devant vous ou dans la cloison placée au-dessus de vous s'ouvrira automatiquement dégageant les inhalateurs d'oxygène. Tenez le masque jaune serré contre vous. Ce geste entraînera l'ouverture automatique de l'embout à oxygène. Appliquez le masque sur votre nez et votre bouche. Fixez le masque au moyen du serre-tête. Respirez normalement. Continuez d'utiliser le masque jusqu'à ce qu'on vous dise de l'enlever. Des masques spéciaux sont prévus pour les enfants. Dans les appareils Caravelle, le personnel de cabine peut fournir des unités portables d'oxygène.

DC-8 — automatisches Sauerstoff-System

Diese Maschinen fliegen in grossen Höhen. Bei plötzlichem Nachlassen des Kabinendrucks ist die sofortige Zufuhr von Sauerstoff erforderlich.
Bei derartiger Änderung des Kabinendrucks öffnet sich automatisch eine Klappe in der Sitzlehne vor Ihnen oder ein Fach über Ihnen, wo Sauerstoffmasken untergebracht sind. Jede einzelne Maske ist durch eine Schnur mit ihrem Sauerstoffventil verbunden. Die gelbe Maske fest ergreifen und zu sich ziehen. Dabei öffnet sich das Ventil automatisch. Maske über Nase und Mund anlegen, und mit dem Halteband befestigen.
Normal atmen. Die Maske anbehalten, bis Anweisungen zum Ablegen erteilt werden. Für Kinder sind Spezialmasken vorhanden. In Caravelle-Maschinen werden lose Sauerstoffgeräte vom Kabinenpersonal ausgegeben.

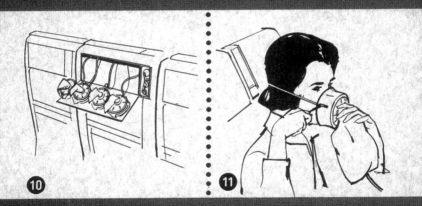

Sistema automático de oxígeno en los DC-8

Estos aviones vuelan a alturas muy elevadas. Si tuviera lugar una disminución brusca de la presión en la cabina el uso de oxígeno será necesario inmediatamente. En caso de tal disminución de la presión se abre automáticamente una portezuela en el respaldo del asiento que tiene delante, o en la pared sobre usted, dejando al descubierto máscaras para respirar oxígeno. Cada máscara está conectada a su válvula por un cordón. Agarre con firmeza la máscara amarilla tirando hacia usted; con ello se abre, automáticamente la válvula de oxígeno. Coloque la máscara sobre la nariz y la boca. Sujete la máscara sobre la cabeza con la cinta.
Respire normalmente. Continúe usando la máscara hasta que le avisen que puede quitársela. Hay máscaras extras para los niños. En los aviones Caravelle el personal de la cabina dispone de unidades portátiles de oxígeno.

SCANDINAVIAN AIRLINES

sas 1386-4

Avión de Propulsión a Chorro, DC-8 de La Eastern

Procedimiento de emergencia para vuelos sobre agua

El avión DC-8 de propulsión a chorro, en el cual Ud. está viajando en estos momentos, es uno de los más poderosos y de mayor confianza que se ha diseñado. Los pilotos y la tripulación han sido estrictamente entrenados y tienen gran experiencia. Hay poca probabilidad de que tengamos que hacer un acuatizaje de emergencia. Sin embargo, queremos familiarizarle con las facilidades que la Eastern ha provisto para su seguridad en casos de emergencia.

LO QUE SE DEBE HACER EN CASOS DE ACUATIZAJE DE EMERGENCIA

1. Siga las instrucciones de la tripulación.
2. Póngase el salvavidas por encima de la cabeza. (Su chaleco salvavidas está en un paquete herméticamente cerrado colocado debajo de cada asiento en la cabina y en el salón "Golden Falcon". No se lo quite excepto en caso de emergencia. Después de ponerse el salvavidas por encima de la cabeza, abróchese las hebillas y amárrelo firmemente por la cintura.)
3. Ponga su asiento en posición vertical y amárrese el cinturón.
4. Antes de que se realice el acuatizaje, échese hacia adelante en su asiento y ponga la cabeza sobre sus piernas, pase los brazos por debajo de las piernas y cójase las manos, poniendo tensos los músculos.
5. Después que el avión se haya detenido, desabotone su cinturón y obedezca las instrucciones de la tripulación para abandonar el avión.
6. Infle su chaleco salvavidas únicamente después que haya abandonado el avión. Se inflará automáticamente después que le haya dado un tirón a las perillas de gas del salvavidas. También se puede inflar por la boca.
7. Obedezca las instrucciones que se le den para abordar los botes salvavidas que serán inflados y botados al agua por la tripulación. Los botes salvavidas están equipados con todas las provisiones necesarias, — alimentos, medicinas, etc.

Este avión mantiene frecuente contacto por radio con el Centro de Control de Vuelo de la Eastern que traza nuestra posición durante el curso del vuelo. En caso de una emergencia, las facilidades de búsqueda serán puestas en vigor inmediatamente.

Las flechas indican las salidas
Los círculos indican la posición de las balsas salvavidas.

Salidas de emergencia.

Los DC-8 están equipados adecuadamente con todas las facilidades de emergencia para en caso de que se necesiten. Las puertas de salida de emergencia están indicadas en el diagrama, izquierda. Todas las puertas están equipadas con desliza- dores de evacuación que se inflan automáticamente, según puede verse abajo. Además, hay ventanas de salida en cada lado de la cabina que pueden ser eliminadas y las cuales tienen las instruc- ciones claramente indicadas y marcadas para que las pueda seguir fácilmente.

Procedimiento para el uso de oxígeno en caso de emergencia.

La falta de atmósfera en grandes altitudes en que se ve forzado a volar el DC-8 requiere que Ud. respire oxígeno en caso de que se pierda la presión concentrada en la cabina; sin embargo, esto es raro que suceda. Su máscara está colocada en un compartimiento en la parte de atrás del asiento que da al pasillo o del asiento del medio. También hay máscaras convenientemente situadas en cada lavatorio y en el salón. Este compartimiento se abre automáticamente si se reduce la presión en la cabina y el oxígeno entrará en la máscara si la presión de la cabina es reducida lo suficientemente para que Ud. obtenga más oxígeno.

QUE SE DEBE HACER EN CASO DE PERDIDA DE PRESION EN LA CABINA

1. Tome la máscara y coloque firmemente el lado abierto sobre su cabeza y amáreselas alrededor de las orejas, nariz y boca; respire normalmente.
2. Pase las tiras elásticas sobre su cabeza y amáreselas alrededor de las orejas.
3. La tripulación le avisará cuando ya no haya necesidad de seguir respirando oxígeno.

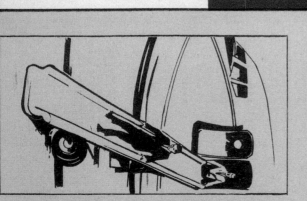

Posición de la máscara de oxígeno

Como sujetarla

EASTERN AIR LINES

Eastern's DC-8 Jet

Emergency Over-Water Flight Procedures

The DC-8 pure jet liner in which you are now flying is one of the most powerful and dependable aircraft ever built. Your pilots and crew are thoroughly skilled and experienced.

There is little likelihood that we will ever be forced to land on the water, but it is good practice to be acquainted with this aircraft's safety provisions.

WHAT TO DO IN CASE OF AN EMERGENCY LANDING ON THE WATER

1. Follow instructions of the crew.
2. Put on life vest over your head.
   (Life vests are located under each seat in the cabin and lounge. Do not remove your vest from its sealed package except in case of a water landing. After fitting the vest over your head, fasten buckles and pull tightly around your waist.)
3. Place your reclining seat in an upright position and fasten your seat belt securely.
4. Before landing on the water, lean forward in your seat and lower your head between your knees; clasp your hands under your legs and tense your muscles.
5. When the aircraft has *completely stopped*, unfasten your seat belt and follow the instructions of the crew for leaving the aircraft.
6. *Inflate your life vest only after you have left the aircraft*. Your life vest is automatically inflated by jerking the gas release knobs on the front of the vest. It may also be inflated orally.
7. Follow instructions for boarding life rafts, which will be launched and inflated by the crew. Life rafts, capable of holding all passengers and crew members, are equipped with all necessary supplies and rations.

ARROWS SHOW EXITS
CIRCLES SHOW LIFE-RAFT LOCATIONS

This aircraft maintains regular and frequent radio contact with Eastern's Flight Control Center, which plots our position throughout the course of our flight. In the event of a water landing, rescue operations would be initiated immediately.

Emergency Exits

Eastern's DC-8's are fully equipped to cope with all possible emergency conditions. Emergency exit doors are indicated in the diagram, left. All exit doors are equipped with automatically inflated evacuation slides, shown below. Also, there are certain removable exit windows on both sides of the cabin that are clearly indicated and marked with simple operating instructions.

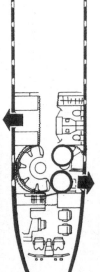

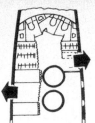

Location of mask

How to hold

Emergency Oxygen System Procedures

The thin air at the high altitudes in which Eastern's DC-8 flies requires that you breathe supplemental oxygen in the event the cabin pressure is lost; however, this occurrence is very unlikely. Your mask is located in a compartment in the aisle seat back or center seat back; mask compartments are also conveniently located in each lavatory and the lounge. The compartment door opens instantly if cabin pressure is reduced, and oxygen will flow through the mask if cabin pressure is reduced enough for you to need supplemental oxygen.

WHAT TO DO IN CASE OF A LOSS OF CABIN PRESSURE

1. Pick up mask and press open side firmly over your nose and mouth; breathe normally.
2. Slip the mask's elastic straps over your head and tighten the straps around your ears.
3. The crew will advise you when there is no need to continue using oxygen.

EASTERN AIR LINES

EAL 14-PR-0016 3-61

PRINTED IN U.S.A.

DC-8

FOR YOUR SAFETY. <u>Know how to move out of this airplane fast.</u> There is fire-danger any time a landing is other than normal—particularly when the airplane structure is damaged.

Below is a floor plan of the plane you are in. Familiarize yourself with the location of the exits. Note particularly the exits nearest you. Study how they are opened and also the protective position you should assume during an emergency landing. When leaving, do not take coats, purses or baggage with you. Move to the exits immediately.

A WORD ABOUT YOUR SEAT BELT—Rough air (turbulence) at high altitudes, although infrequent, can be severe. When seat belt sign is lighted in-flight, please comply with the sign immediately to prevent possible injury. Experienced air travelers usually keep their seat belts fastened <u>all the time</u> when seated.

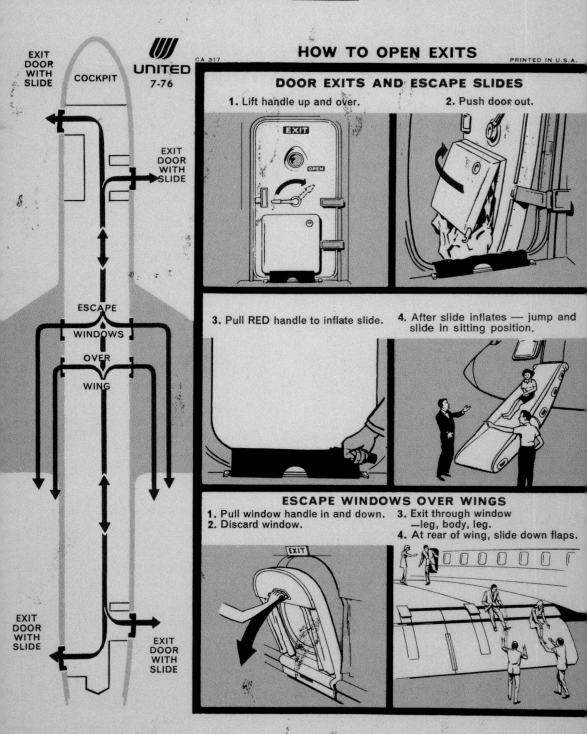

EXIT DOOR WITH SLIDE

COCKPIT

UNITED
7-76

CA 317

EXIT DOOR WITH SLIDE

ESCAPE WINDOWS OVER WING

EXIT DOOR WITH SLIDE

EXIT DOOR WITH SLIDE

HOW TO OPEN EXITS

PRINTED IN U.S.A.

DOOR EXITS AND ESCAPE SLIDES

1. Lift handle up and over.

2. Push door out.

EXIT
OPEN

3. Pull RED handle to inflate slide.

4. After slide inflates — jump and slide in sitting position.

ESCAPE WINDOWS OVER WINGS

1. Pull window handle in and down.
2. Discard window.

3. Exit through window —leg, body, leg.
4. At rear of wing, slide down flaps.

EXIT

HOW TO USE THE OXYGEN MASK

Jet aircraft fly at high altitude and the cabin is pressurized for your comfort. If cabin pressure ever was lost, you would be breathing high altitude "thin" air...so it is imperative that *cigars and cigarettes be extinguished immediately and oxygen masks be put on as shown below.*

1. WHERE TO LOCATE MASKS.
Oxygen masks are in a compartment in the center seat back of three place seats and the aisle seat back of two place seats. In the lounges, masks are located in ceiling or wall compartments. If oxygen is ever required, compartment doors open automatically.

2. HOW TO USE MASKS.
Remain seated. Grasp nearest mask and *pull it from its holder.* A cord turns oxygen on as you pull mask to you.

For children's use, a spare mask is available at each row.

3. UNCOIL OXYGEN TUBE AND PLASTIC BAG.
The coiled oxygen tube, plastic bag, and head band are stored inside the mask and should be lifted out. The oxygen supply tube is long enough to permit you to relax comfortably in your seat.

4. HOW TO ADJUST MASKS FOR COMFORT.
Once mask is in position, it may be easily adjusted for comfortable fit. If too tight, hold mask in position and pull gently on elastic head band with free hand. If too loose, pull tabs located where head band connects to mask. Do not overtighten, as this may misshape mask and cause discomfort.

PROTECTIVE POSITIONS

Sit well back in seat — Pull seat belt tight.
Assume position in illustration — Keep position until plane stops.

Forward Facing Seat

Sign in front of you tells which cushion is floatable.

Rear Facing Seat

If bottom cushion—
Grasp it at back.
Pull it up HARD.
Flip it over onto floor.
Step on it to detach.

If lower back cushion —
Grasp it at top.
Pull it forward HARD to detach.

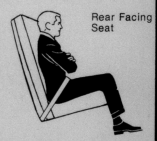

VIASA

Fig. 1

Fig. 2

Fig. 3

Fig. 4

NORMAS DE SEGURIDAD

De acuerdo con los reglamentos internacionales este avión está dotado con todos los medios de seguridad adecuado a las exigencias de toda línea aérea.

En caso de dificultad durante el viaje, le rogamos permanezca tranquilo y tenga la seguridad de que la tripulación ha sido perfectamente adiestrada para el empleo de todos los medios de socorro y le dará las instrucciones que deberá usted seguir sin alarmarse y con la máxima escrupulosidad.

En el momento del aviso, tome usted las precauciones siguientes: quítese las gafas, collares, corbata y cualquier objeto que esté en contacto con el cuello; desabróchese así mismo el cuello de la camisa. Saque de los bolsillos todo objeto agudo, como lápices metálicos, etc. (Fig. 1).

Coloque el respaldo del asiento en posición perfectamente vertical.

Mantenga bien apretado el cinturón de seguridad.

Apoye los pies en el soporte del asiento delantero.

Apoye los brazos cruzados en el respaldo del asiento delantero y descanse la cabeza sobre éstos, o coloque sobre sus rodillas una almohada, una manta doblada o algo similar y encima apoye la cabeza, y, manteniendo los codos bajos, junte las manos detrás de la nuca (Fig. 2); mantenga la tensión muscular a fin de

soportar mejor un posible choque. Tan solo cuando el avión esté completamente parado desátese el cinturón y diríjase con calma hacia las salidas de emergencia. Podrá usted apreciar donde se encuentran, observando el esquema del tipo de avión, en el interior de la cabina existen además inscripciones que le permitirán localizar cada salida de emergencia.

La tripulación procederá a señalar y ayudarle a abandonar la nave por las salidas de emergencia, le rogamos encarecidamente permanezca tranquilo.

En caso de amaraje, quítese los zapatos, si son de tacón alto o con suela claveteada, y prepare el salvavidas. Póngaselo (Fig. 3), sujete los tirantes (Fig. 4) y tírelos fuertemente hasta conseguir que el salvavidas adhiera al cuerpo (Fig. 5); a los niños colóquese las correas entre las piernas y tiren luego de la forma indicada anteriormente.

No infle el salvavidas hasta que haya salido del avión (Fig. 6) para inflarlo, tire del cordón situados en la extremidad de las cámaras de aire (Fig. 7). De no inflarse el salvavidas con este sistema sople con fuerza en los tubos de goma (Fig. 8). Cierre luego las válvulas y siga las instrucciones dadas por la tripulación y quien pondrá en función los medios de socorro colectivo.

Si se abriera, ante usted (Fig. 9) el depósito que contiene la máscara de oxígeno, aplíqueselo rápidamente respirando normalmente.

ESTA TERMINANTEMENTE PROHIBIDO FUMAR MIENTRAS ESTE RESPIRANDO OXIGENO.

DC - 8

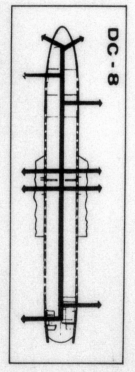

EMERGENCY INSTRUCTIONS

In accordance with international regulations this aircraft is provided with safety equipment adapted to each particular type of flight.

In case of difficulty, please, remain calm. Your crew has been carefully trained to use first aid means and will give you suitable instructions which you are expected to put into practice with scrupulous care and without being alarmed.

As soon as the alarm is given take the following precautions: remove glasses, necklaces and any object in touch with the neck; unbutton collar, remove from pockets all sharp objects such as metal pencils (Fig. 1).

Bring the back of the chair in a perfectly vertical position again. Fasten safety belt.

Place your feet on the footrest of the chair in front of you. Put your forehead on your forearms crossed on the back of the chair in front of you or put a pillow or a folded blanket or coat on your knees, your head on it and join your hands behind your neck keeping your elbows down (Fig. 2) keep your muscles taut to absorb a possible impact.

Only when the aircraft has completely stopped, unfasten your safety belt and move calmy towards the emergency exits. You can see where they are if you study the accompanying diagrams. All exits are, clearly marked inside the aircraft cabin. In case of emergency, these exits are opened by the cabin staff just before landing to enable everyone to get out as quickly as possible. Please remain calm!

Fig. 5

Fig. 6

EMERGENCY E...

Fig. 7

Fig. 8

Fig. 9

If you are wearing high-heeled or hobnailed shoes take them off in case of ditching and prepare your life-jacket. Put it on (Fig. 3) fasten the straps (Fig. 4) and pull them out until the lifejacket fits closely (Fig. 5); on children, straps should be fitted under their legs and pulled as above.

Do not inflate lifejacket before leaving the aircraft (Fig. 6).

Inflate lifejacket by pulling the strings of the two flasks (Fig. 7).

If lifejacket does not inflate, blow some air through the rubber tubes (Fig. 8), then close valves tightly and follow the instructions given by the crew who will operate the collective aid means.

Should the compartment containing the oxygen mask open in front of you, pick up the mask quickly and apply it to the face (Fig. 9). DO NOT SMOKE.

While taking oxygen DO NOT SMOKE.

CONSIGNES DE SÉCURITÉ

Conformément aux règlements internationaux, cet avion est pourvu d'équipements de sécurité adaptés aux exigences de chaque service.

En cas de difficultés, restez calmes, votre équipage est parfaitement entraîné à l'emploi de tous les moyens de secours et vous donnera des ordres nécessaires que vous devrez suivre strictement et sans vous alarmer.

Dès que l'annonce en est donnée, prenez les precautions suivantes: enlevez lunettes, cravate, collier avec que tout autre objet en contact avec le cou; desserrez votre col, videz vos poches de tout objet pointu, crayons métalliques etc. (Fig. 1).

Ramenez le dossier de votre siège dans la position parfaitement verticale.

Bouclez votre ceinture de siège, en serrant bien.

Posez vos pieds sur le support du fauteuil devant vous.

Appuyez votre front sur vos avant-bras après les avoir croisés sur le dossier du fauteuil devant vous, ou bien posez un coussin, une couverture pliée ou un semblable vêtement sur vos genoux, appuyez-y la tête et joignez vos mains derrière la nuque en tenant les coudes abaissés (Fig. 2); tendez vos muscles pour mieux supporter un choc eventuel.

Attendez l'immobilisation complete de l'avion pour déboucler votre ceinture de siège, approchez vous ensuite avec calme de l'issue de secours.

Celles-ci sont facilement repérables sur le croquis du type d'avion à bord duquel vous volez et sont, en outre, clairement indiquées à l'intérieur même de la cabine. En cas d'atterrissage forcé, le personnel de bord ouvrira les issues de secours.

Nous vous prions de conserver votre sang-froid.

En cas d'amerrissage, ôtez aussi vos chaussures, si elles sont à talons hauts ou à semelles cloutées, et préparez votre gilet de sauvetage.

Enfilez-le (Fig. 3), fixez-en les sangles (Fig. 4) et tirez-les le plus possible en dehors, jusqu'à avoir le gilet bien adhérent à votre corps (Fig. 5); pour les enfants, faites leur passer les jambes à travers le bretelles et opérez comme ci-dessus.

Ne gonflez pas votre gilet avant d'avoir quitté l'avion (Fig. 6); pour le gonfler tirer les cordonnets des bombes d'oxygène (Fig. 7). Si le gilet ne se gonfle pas, soufflez dans les tubes en cautochouc (Fig. 8), fermez ensuite les soupapes et suivez les instructions de l'équipage qui mettra en oeuvre les moyens de secours collectif.

Si la boîte à masque s'ouvre devant vous, prendre rapidement un masque et l'appliquer sur le visage (Fig. 9).

Pendant la diffusion de l'oxygène il est STRICTEMENT DÉFENDU DE FUMER.

ISTRUZIONI PER L'USO

In conformità ai regolamenti internazionali questo aereo è dotato di mezzi di sicurezza adeguati alle esigenze di ogni linea.

In caso di difficoltà restate calmi, il vostro equipaggio è perfettamente addestrato all'impiego di ogni mezzo di soccorso e vi darà gli ordini opportuni che dovrete seguire con scrupolosità e senza allarmarvi.

Appena vi viene dato l'annuncio prendete le seguenti precauzioni: toglietevi gli occhiali, cravatta, collane e qualsiasi altro oggetto a contatto del collo; sbottonatevi il colletto; toglietevi dalle tasche ogni oggetto acuminato, matite metalliche ecc. (Fig. 1).

Riportate la spalliera della poltrona in posizione perfettamente verticale.

Allacciate strettamente la cintura di sicurezza.

Appoggiate i piedi sul supporto della poltrona davanti alla vostra.

Appoggiate la fronte sugli avambracci incrociati sulla spalliera che vi sta davanti, o mettete un cuscino, una coperta piegata o alcunché di simile sulle ginocchia, appoggiatevi sopra la testa e congiungete le mani dietro la nuca tenendo i gomiti abbassati (Fig. 2); tendete i muscoli per sopportare meglio un eventuale urto.

Solo quando gli l'aereo è completamente fermo, slacciate la cintura ed avviatevi con calma verso le uscite di sicurezza. Potete facilmente rendervi conto dove si trovano esaminando il disegno del tipo di aereo sul quale state volando; inoltre vi sono scritte all'interno della cabina che vi permettono di individuarle.

In caso di necessità il personale di cabina provvederà alla apertura delle uscite di sicurezza; vi preghiamo di restare calmi.

In caso di ammaraggio, toglietevi anche le scarpe se a tacco alto o con suola chiodata e preparate il salvagente. Infilatelo (Fig. 3), agganciate le bretelle (Fig. 4) e tiratele fuori, fino ad avere il salvagente bene aderente al corpo (Fig. 5); ai bambini fate passare le bretelle sotto le gambe e tenderele come sopra.

Non gonfiate il salvagente finché non siete usciti dall'aereo (Fig. 6); per gonfiarlo tirate i cordoncini delle bombolette (Fig.7). Se con tale sistema il salvagente non si gonfia, soffiate negli appositi tubi di gomma (Fig. 8) chiudete quindi le valvole, e seguite le disposizioni impartite dall'equipaggio, che metterà in funzione i mezzi collettivi di soccorso.

Se vedete aprirsi davanti a voi lo scomparto contenente le maschere per l'ossigeno, afferrate rapidamente una maschera ed applicatela al viso, respirando normalmente (Fig. 9).

Per tutto il periodo in cui respirate ossigeno NON FUMATE.

Douglas
DC-8
Model 62

Safety instructions

Instructions de sécurité

Sicherheits-Instruktionen

Istruzioni di sicurezza

Instrucciones de seguridad

Instruções de segurança

Sept. 67

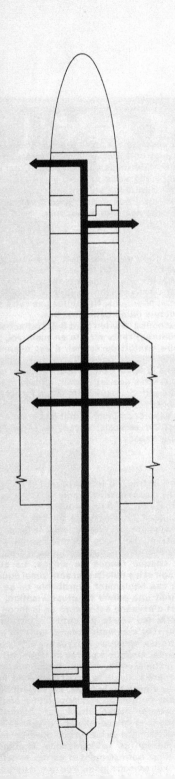

Emergency Exit
Sortie de secours
Notausgang
Uscita di emergenza
Salida de emergencia
Saída de emergência

Page 93. JAL, Douglas DC-8. This was the first card for JAL Douglas DC-8 and is from the early 1960s.

Page 95. Air Afrique, Douglas DC-8. A card from the 1960s.

Page 97. ONA, Douglas DC-8. This card is from the early 1960s.

Page 99. SAS, Douglas DC-8, CV-440 Metropolitan, DC-7C, Caravelle and CV-990 Coronado. This "Fleet card" is from the late 1960s.

Page 101. Eastern, Douglas DC-8. This is probably the first Eastern DC-8 card, dating from 1961.

Page 103. United, Douglas DC-8. This card is from 1976.

Page 105. Viasa, Douglas DC-8. A card from the mid-1970s.

Page 107. Swissair, Douglas DC-8. This card dates from 1967. Text-style cards were replaced by more graphics-oriented ones in 1969.

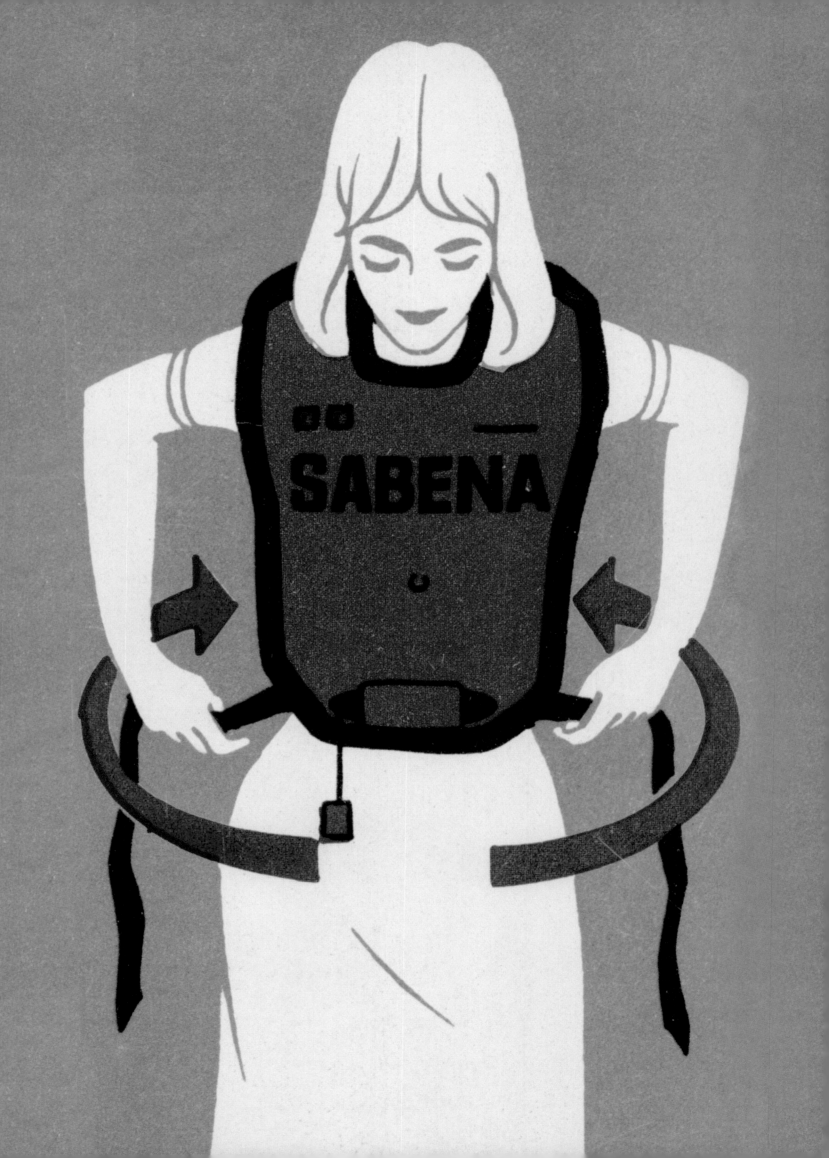

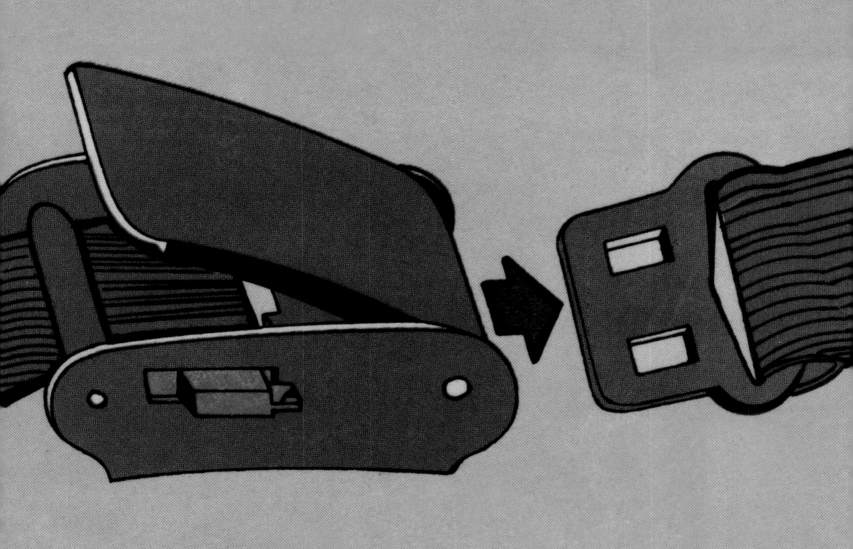

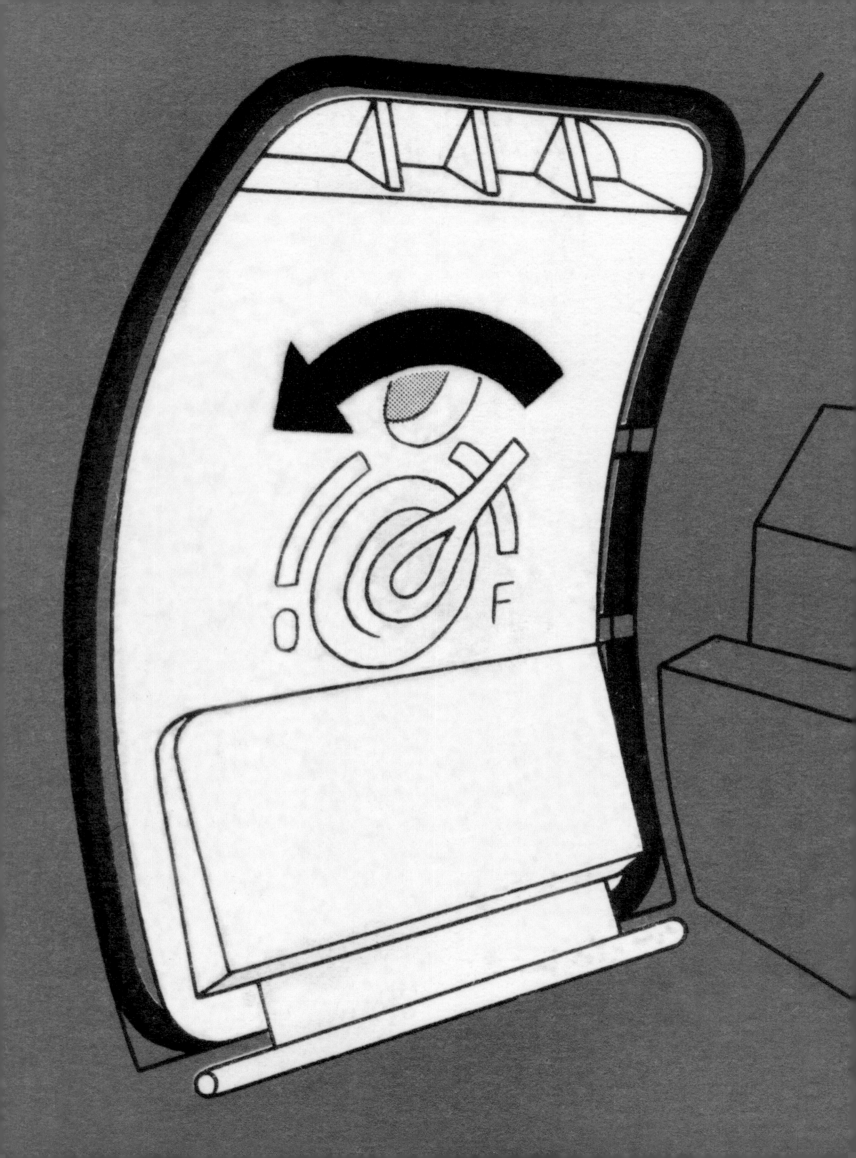

The Convair 880

The success of the Boeing 707 and the Douglas DC-8 made other manufacturers explore jet technology further. An interesting example of a project that did not go so well is the General Dynamics Convair 880. When introduced in 1960, the "Coronado", as it was called, became touted as the fastest airliner of its time. The Coronado went down like a lead balloon when it turned out that maintaining that speed meant guzzling fuel.

Convair safety cards are very typical of the 1960s. They are quite rare, since the aircraft itself was very short-lived, used by just a few airlines.

In April 1956, the Convair division of U.S. company General Dynamics announced the production of a medium-range jet transport. The project was first called Skylark, and later the Golden Arrow. Then the name was changed again to Convair 600, referring to its speed of 600 miles (965 km) per hour, equivalent to 880 feet (268 metres) per second, which led to the final name of Convair 880. The aircraft cruised at around .87 Mach, which is considerably faster than today's airliners, except, of course, for the Concorde, making it the fastest airliner built in the United States.

The model 22 made its maiden journey on 27 January 1959. The later 22-m model was in the air on 3 October 1960. The Convair 990 was a stretched version of the 880, also appearing in the early 1960s.

The first airline to fly the Convair 880 was Delta, in May 1960, but sales of the plane were slow – it was quite costly to purchase, did not have the capacity of the 707 or DC-8, and also became known as less than fuel-efficient. The Coronado broke many speed records for passenger planes and it still holds some today, but that did not make it a commercial success. The major airlines had all discontinued flying the Coronado by 1974. One of the few remaining 880s is Elvis Presley's private jet, "Lisa Marie", which is on display at Graceland, Elvis's home in Memphis, Tennessee.

LANICA

OVER-WATER FLIGHT PROCEDURES

GETTING READY

If you are given the order to "prepare for ditching", empty your pockets of all sharp objects. Take off your glasses, tie or high-heeled shoes.

TO PUT ON YOUR LIFE VEST

A life vest is provided under your seat. To put it on:

❶ Slip it on over your head.

❷ Fasten the rings on the waist strap ends to the snaps at the bottom front of the vest; grasp the pull tabs on the waist strap ends and pull snug around your waist.

❸ As you leave the airplane, inflate the life vest by pulling sharply on the two cords at the bottom.

❹ If the vest becomes deflated later, depress mouthpiece and blow.

EMERGENCY LANDING ON WATER

A After your life vest is on, put your seat forward in the upright position, and fasten the seat belt.

B Lean forward, place your head on your knees.

C Wait for instructions before leaving the airplane and stepping into the life raft.

D Inflate your life vest only when you leave the airplane. A crew member will tell you when.

E Radio communications have already started rescue.

Your crew will show you the emergency exits. Do not leave your seat before the airplane has come to a stop. All you have to do is follow instructions carefully and keep calm.

❶   ❷   ❸   ❹

NORMAS DE NE EN VUELOS SOBRE EL MAR

ESTE PREPARADO

Si se le ordenara prepararse para amatar, vacíe sus bolsillos de objetos puntragudos, quítese las gatas y la corbata. También sus zapatos, si tienen los tacones altos.

SU CHALECO SALVAVIDAS

Hay un chaleco salvavidas debajo de su asiento para ponérselo:

❶ Deslízeselo sobre la cabeza.

❷ Enganche las anillas del cinturón en los corchetes de la parte inferior delantera del chaleco, después sujete las tiras del cinturón y ajústeselo bien a la cintura.

❸ Al momento de abandonar el avión infie el chaleco tirando rapidamente de los dos cordones de la parte inferior.

❹ Si el chaleco pierde aire afloje la boquilla y sopie por ella.

AMARAJE FORZOSO

A Después de haberse puesto el chaleco salvavidas coloque su asiento hacia delante en posición recta y átese el cinturón de su butaca.

B Inclínese hacia delante descansando la cabeza sobre sus rodillas.

C Espere a que un miembro de la tripulación le de instrucciones de como ha de abandonar el avión.

D Debe esperar para inflar su chaleco hasta que un miembro de la tripulación selo ordene.

E La comunicación por radio habrá ya empezado las tareas para su salvamento.

Su tripulación le mostrará las salidas de emergencia. Por favor no se mueva de su sitio. Lo unico que ud. Tiene que hacer es atenerse a estas instrucciones y manterse sereno.

LIFE RAFTS

This aircraft carries 4 life rafts with 25-man capacity and 1 life raft with 15-man capacity which will accommodate all passengers and crew members in the event of an emergency landing on water. In all instances, your flight crew will launch and inflate the life rafts.

LOCATION OF LIFE RAFTS AND EMERGENCY EXITS

- • Circles show position of life rafts.
- ➤ Arrows show emergency exits.

WINDOW EXITS

1. Pull handle in.
2. Lift window free of opening.
3. Turn on side and throw out.

Flotation Seat Cushions:
The cushion on which you are sitting is designed to keep you afloat. In the event of a water landing, grasp the cushion at the rear, pull it forward and take it with you.

HOW TO USE EMERGENCY OXYGEN

Jet flights are normally conducted above 25,000 ft. with the cabin pressurized to an altitude of 5,000 ft. to 8,000 ft. If the cabin pressure is suddenly lost, you are at the same altitude as the aircraft and it is imperative lighted cigarettes be extinguished immediately and oxygen masks be put on as indicated below.

1. **Where to locate masks.** The oxygen masks are located in the overhead panel. Whenever additional oxygen is required, the door covering the masks will automatically open.

2. **How to use masks.** Take nearest mask firmly and pull toward you. As mask is pulled from the compartment, a cord will be pulled free allowing the oxygen to flow.

3. **Fitting of mask.** Remove oxygen tube and plastic bag from inside mask. Place mask over nose and mouth holding it in place with one hand. Slip the headband over your head. This will hold oxygen mask in proper position.

4. **Mask adjustment for comfortable fit.** Once the mask is in position, it may be easily adjusted. If too tight, hold the mask in position and pull gently on elastic headband with free hand. If too loose, pull tabs located where headband connects to mask as shown. Do not overtighten as this may misshape mask and cause discomfort.

BRACING POSITION

In the event a non-routine landing is anticipated, you will be directed to assume the position depicted on the illustration below. 1. Fasten seat belt securely. 2. Place both feet together on the floor directly in front of you. 3. Lean over and rest your head on your knees. 4. Clasp hands firmly under legs. Remain in this position until the aircraft comes to a complete stop.

DOOR EXITS & ESCAPE SLIDES

1. Lift handle up.
2. Push door out.
3. Open slide compartment door, slide will inflate.
4. Sit on slide.

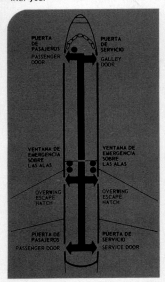

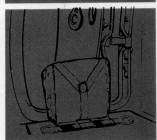

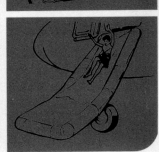

SALIDAS DE EMERGENCIA

En la ilustración interior se muestra la ubicación de las salidas de emergencia existentes en el avión CV-880. Le suplicamos se familiarice con ellas, particularmente con la más cercana a usted. Al abandonar el avión, diríjase inmediatamente a las salidas y no se detenga ni regrese por pertenencias personales.

VENTANILLAS DE SALIDA DE EMERGENCIA

1. Tire de la manija.
2. Levante la ventanilla para sacaria del marco.
3. Dele vuelta de lado y arrójela al vacío.

Cojin Flotador
El cojin en que está sentado fué diseñado para mantenerie a flote. En caso de amarizaje, tire de él por su parte posterior y llévelo consigo.

POSTURA DE PROTECCION

En caso de presentarse un aterrizaje de emergencia, se le darán instrucciones para que adopte la postura ilustrada en el grabado. 1. Abróchese fuertemente el cinturón de seguridad. 2. Junte los piés en el piso, directamente frente a usted. 3. Inclínese y apoye la cabeza en las rodillas. 4. Enlace firmemente las manos bajo las piernas. Manténgase en esa postura hasta que el avión se detenga por completo.

PUERTAS DE EMERGENCIA Y DESLIZADORES DE ESCAPE

1. Levante la manija.
2. Empuje la puerto.
3. Tire del asa para inflar el deslizador.
4. Salte y siéntese en el deslizador.

COMO USAR LAS MASCARILLAS DE OXIGENO

Los vuelos en jet normalmente se realizan a alturas superiores a los 25,000 piés, mientras que la presión atmosférica de la cabina se mantiene entre 5,000 y 8,000 piés. Si de pronto se perdiera la presión de la cabina, los pasajeros se encontrarían a la misma presión atmosférica que el avión, lo que haría imperativo apagar de inmediato los cigarillos y usar las mascarillas de oxígeno como a continuación se indica.

1. **Ubicacion de las mascarillas.** Las mascarillas se encuentran en el tablero situado directamente arriba de los asientos. En el momento en que empiece a faltar oxígeno, la puerta que oculta las mascarillas se abrirá automáticamente.

2. **Como usar las mascarillas.** Tome firmemente la mascarilla más cercana y tire de ella hacia usted. Al tirar de la mascarilla, se soltará el tubo alimentador y el oxígeno fluirá.

3. **Ajuste de la mascarilla.** Saque el tubo alimentador y la bolsa de plástico del interior de la mascarilla. Colóquese la mascarilla sobre la nariz y boca, sosteniéndola en su sitio con una mano. Pase la cinta elástica por atrás de la cabeza. Así la mantendrá en su sitio.

4. **Como ajustar la mascarilla a su medida.** Una vez que la mascarilla esté en su sitio, puede ajustarse fácilmente. Si está demasiado ajustada, sosténgala en su lugar y tire suavemente de la cinta elástica. Si está demasiado holgada, tire de la agujetas del cinta elástica (vea ilustración). No la ajuste en demasía, ya que ello podría deformar la mascarilla y originarie incomodidades.

For sikkerhets skyld

Turvallisuus

Safety on board

SIKKERHET OMBORD

Alt er gjort for at Deres reise skal bli behagelig og sikker. Besetningen har gjennomgått en mangeårig, effektiv utdannelse. Flyet blir konstant gjennomprøvet og kontrollert til minste detalj av erfarne teknikere. Det er forsynt med moderne navigasjonsinstrumenter og dessuten utrustet med betryggende sikkerhetsforanstaltninger. For å forsikre oss om at denne utrustningen blir benyttet på rette måte, vil vi imidlertid be Dem rette Deres oppmerksomhet på følgende regler og forskrifter.

DERES STOL

er forsynt med sikkerhetsbelte, som holder Dem fast i stolen om det skulle bli nødvendig å fly gjennom dårlig vær, eller om en nødsituasjon skulle oppstå. Sikkerhetsbeltet har en låseanordning som er meget lett å betjene. Spennet må imidlertid trykkes ordentlig ned for å kunne låse beltet sikkert. For ikke å skade maven bør sikkerhetsbeltet plaseres rundt hoften.
Sikkerhetsbeltet skal alltid være spent ved start og landing, samt når flyet går gjennom dårlig vær. Kapteinen meddeler dette ved å tende skiltet »FASTEN SEAT BELT«.

RØYKING

er ikke tillatt under start og landing. Flyets kaptein meddeler Dem dette ved å tende skiltet »NO SMOKING«.

NØDUTGANGER

er tydelig merket som vist på fig. 1-2-3. Flyskissen på fig. 4 viser hvor De kan finne nødutgangene.

TURVALLISUUS

Olemme tehneet kaikkemme, jotta matkanne olisi miellyttävä ja turvallinen. Miehistö on saanut tehokkaan koulutuksen, kokenut ja hyvin koulutettu kenttähenkilökunta on tehnyt yleiskatsauksen ja tarkastanut lentokoneen pienintä yksityiskohtaa myöten. Siinä on nykyaikaiset ohjauslaitteet ja se on lisäksi varustettu varmoilla turvallisuuslaitteilla. Varmistautuaksemme siitä, että näitä varusteita käytetään oikealla tavalla, haluamme kiinnittää huomionne seuraaviin ohjeisiin ja määräyksiin.

ISTUIMENNE

on varustettu turvavyöllä, joka pysyttää Teidät tuolissa, jos olisi välttämätöntä lentää huonolla säällä tai jos jouduttaisiin vaaralliseen tilanteeseen. Turvavyössä on lukkolaite, jota on hyvin helppo käsitellä. Solki on kuitenkin painettava alas kunnollisesti, jotta vyö saataisiin varmasti lukkoon. Vatsan vahingoittumisen välttämiseksi on turvavyö asetettava tarpeeksi alas lantion ympärille. Turvavyön tulee aina olla kiinnitetty koneen noustessa ja laskeutuessa sekä huonon sään aikana. Kapteeni ilmoittaa asiasta sytyttämällä valon ilmoitustauluun »FASTEN SEAT BELT«.

TUPAKOIMINEN

ei ole sallittu nousun ja laskeutumisen aikana. Kapteeni ilmoittaa asiasta sytyttämällä valon ilmoitustauluun »NO SMOKING«.

VARAULOSKÄYTÄVÄT

on selvästi merkitty, kuten kuva 1-2-3 osoittaa. Lentokoneluonnokset kuv. 4 osoittavat, missä varauloshäytävät sijaitsevat.

SAFETY ON BOARD

Every possible effort is being made to make your voyage comfortable and safe. Your crew has been trained to the utmost efficiency, your airplane has been overhauled and checked to its smallest components, by experienced ground personnel and the airplane is provided with the best instruments and safety devices available. In order to have this equipment used properly we have to ask you, however, to follow the rules and regulations given.

YOUR SEAT

is provided with a seat belt which holds you down in the seat, should it be necessary to fly through gusty weather or should an emergency arise. The seat belt has a buckle which is very easy and quick to secure or release. The buckle must, however, be pressed firmly down to be positively locked. In order not to hurt your stomach place the belt around your hip-bones. The seat belt shall always be fastened during take-off and landing and when flying in gusty winds. The captain will inform you about this by lighting the sign »FASTEN SEAT BELT«.

SMOKING

is not permitted during take-off and landing. The captain will inform you about this by lighting the sign »NO SMOKING«.

EMERGENCY EXITS

are clearly marked as shown on fig. 1-2-3 and located as shown in fig. 4.

fig. 1

fig. 2

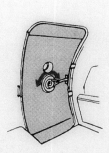

fig. 3

fig. 4

NØDINSTRUKSJON

»GJØR KLAR FOR NØDLANDING«!
Denne ordre gis av besetningen, hvis det skulle bli nødvendig å utføre en nødlanding. De skal da:

1. Fjerne briller (glasögon), eventuelt gebiss (löständer, protese), og alle skarpe gjenstander som blyant, penn, nåler, smykker etc.
2. Løsne på slips og trange krager.
3. Ta av høyhelte sko.
4. Ta på redningsvesten hvis ikke annen ordre gis.
   OBS! BLÅS (PUST) DEN IKKE OPP.
5. Sette stolryggen i loddrett stilling.
6. Spenne sikkerhetsbeltet rundt hoften og avvent ytterligere instrukser.
   Forberedelsene til en nødlanding kan ta 10—20 minutter, og først deretter kommer den neste ordre:

»VÆR FORBEREDT PÅ STØT« (»Brace for Impact«). Denne ordre gis 1—2 minutter før selve landingen. De skal da:

1. Bøye Dem fremover med pannen hvilende mot armene, som De holder korslagt på knærne.
2. Bli sittende i denne stilling helt til flyet har stoppet fullstendig.
3. Da — men heller ikke før — kan De løsne sikkerhetsbeltet og forlate flyet. De må hele tiden nøye følge alle instruksjoner fra flyets besetning.

HUSK AT DE SKAL:

1. Holde Dem i ro og følge nøye gitte instruksjoner.
2. Sitte foroverbøyd til flyet har stoppet helt.
3. Blås (pust) aldri opp redningsvesten før De har forlatt flyet.
4. Benytt den nødutgang De er blitt anvist.

HÄTÄOHJEITA

»VALMISTAUTUKAA PAKKOLAS-KUUN!« Tämän käskyn antaa miehistö, jos pakkolaskun suorittaminen, osoittautuu välttämättömäksi. Silloin Teidän on huomioitava seuraavat asiat:

1. Poistakaa silmälasit, hammasproteesit ja terävät esineet, kuten kynät, neulat, korut j. n. e.
2. Höllentäkää kaulus ja kaulahuivi.
3. Riisukaa korkeakorkoiset kengät.
4. Pukekaa päällenne pelastusliivit, ellei muuta määräystä anneta.
   HUOM! Älkää puhaltako niihin ilmaa!
5. Asettakaa tuolien selkänojat pystyasentoon.
6. Kiinnittäkää pelastusvyö lantioille ja odottakaa lisäohjeita. Laskeutumisvalmistelut kestävät 10—20 min. ja vasta senjälkeen tulee seuraava määräys:

»SUOJAUTUKAA PAKKOLASKUA VARTEN!« Tämä määräys annetaan 1—2 min. ennen kuin kone on maassa. Silloin Teidän on tehtävä seuraavat asiat:

1. Kumartukaa eteenpäin niin, että otsa nojaa käsivarsiin, jotka pidätte ristissä polvien päällä.
2. Jääkää istumaan siten siksi kunnes lentokone on pysähtynyt.
3. Vasta nyt voitte irroittaa turvavyön ja poistua lentokoneesta. Seuratkaa tarkoin miehistön ohjeita ja määräyksiä.

MUISTAKAA SEURAAVAT ASIAT:

1. Olkaa rauhallinen ja seuratkaa annettuja määräyksiä.
2. Jääkää istumaan eteenpäin kumartuneena siksi, kunnes kone on pysähtynyt tyystin.
3. Pelastusliivejä ei koskaan saa täyttää ilmalla ennen koneesta poistumista.
4. Käyttäkää Teille neuvottua varauloskäytävää.

EMERGENCY PROCEDURES

»PREPARE FOR EMERGENCY LANDING!« This is the first order you will receive should it be necessary to make an emergency landing. You must then:

1. Remove glasses, false teeth and sharp objects such as pencils, clips etc.
2. Loosen collar and necktie.
3. Take off high-heeled shoes.
4. Put on your life jacket unless otherwise ordered. DO NOT INFLATE.
5. Set the back of your seat in the vertical position.
6. Fasten your seat belt securely around your hips and await further orders. It will now take 10—20 minutes for landing preparations and the second order is given:

»BRACE FOR IMPACT!« This order is given 1—2 minutes before landing. You must then:

1. Lean forward cradling your head in folded arms on your knees.
2. Hold the position until the aircraft has come to rest. Two or more bumps are felt before the aircraft finally comes to rest.
3. Now, and not before, you may release your safety belt and leave the aircraft, following the orders of the crew.

REMEMBER THAT YOU MUST:

1. Keep calm and follow given orders.
2. Be seated leaning forward until the plane has stopped completely.
3. Never inflate your life jacket inside the plane.
4. Use the exit assigned to you.

DERES REDNINGSVEST

er plasert under stolen. Redningsvesten må ikke blåses (pustes) opp før De har forlatt flyet.

PELASTUSLIIVINNE

ovat oman tuolinne alla. Liivejä ei saa täyttää ilmalla ennen koneesta poistumista.

YOUR LIFE VEST

is placed below your seat. Never inflate your life jacket inside the plane.

Trekk redningsvesten over hodet.
Vetäkää pelastusliivit pään yli.
Put on the life jacket over your head.

Fest bakstykkets stropper til krokene på forstykket. Trekk i stroppene og stram.
Kiinnittäkää takakappaleen nauhat edessä olevien pitimiin. Kiinnittäkää liivit vetämällä nauhojen päistä.
Connect the straps to the hooks and tighten by pulling the ends.

Redningsvesten blåses (pustes) automatisk opp ved å trekke i de to kullsyrebeholderes utløsningssnor.
Pelastusliivit täyttyvät automaattisesti silloin, kun vedetään hiilihapposäiliöiden laukaisunuorista.
The life jacket is inflated by releasing the CO₂ capsules.

Redningsvesten kan også blåses (pustes) opp gjennom de to munnstykkene.
Pelastusliivit voidaan täyttää ilmalla puhaltamalla molempiin suuttimiin.
The life jacket can also be inflated by blowing into the mouthpieces.

TA DET ROLIG (LUGNT)

Nødlandinger er ytterst sjeldne nåtildags. Men man må være forberedt på alle eventualiteter. Våre besetninger trenes periodisk på å kunne møte nødsituasjoner og hvert besetningsmedlem vet i detalj hvordan alle eventualiteter skal møtes. Skulle en situasjon inntreffe (hvilket er høyst usannsynlig) — som krever nødlanding: FORHOLD DEM ROLIG (LUGNT) og følg besetningens instruksjoner.

Hvor det er påkrevet medfølger et antall gummibåter, som er plasert på den dertil innrettede plass i kabinen.
På flyvninger over polar- eller ørkenområder medfører flyet spesielt nødutstyr for disse strøk.

PYSYKÄÄ RAUHALLISENA

Pakkolaskut ovat nykyisin äärettömän harvinaisia. Mutta täytyy olla varautunut kaiken varalta. Miehistöämme harjoitetaan säännöllisin väliajoin myöskin hätätilanteita silmällä pitäen Ja jokainen miehistöön kuuluva tietää yksityiskohtia myöten, miten suhtautua kaikkiin tapauksiin. Jos jouduttaisiin tilanteeseen — mikä on hyvin epätodellista — joka vaatisi pakkolaskun, niin: PYSYKÄÄ RAUHALLISENA ja seuratkaa miehistön ohjeita.

Mikäli pelastuslauttoja tarvittaisiin, on niitä riittävä määrä matkustamon pelastuslauttaosasto(i)ssa.
Lentokone kuljetaa napa- tai erämaa-alueiden yli lennettäessä erikoista pakkotila varustusta näitä alueita varten.

STAY CALM

Emergency landings are extremely rare nowadays. Our crews, however, are continuously trained also to meet with emergency situations, and every crew member knows in detail how to act. Should a situation arise (which is most unlikely) requiring an emergency landing: KEEP CALM and follow all instructions given by the crew.

If life rafts are required, a number of rubber dinghies with adequate space are carried in the liferaft compartment(s).
On routes via polar or desert regions the aircraft will carry special emergency equipment for these regions.

Page 115. Lanica. Convair 880. These cards are based on the format used by Air West (the predecessor to Hughes Airwest). Lanica operated several second-hand CV-880s from Nicaragua to Miami in the mid-1970s

Page 117. InterNord, Convair 990. This card was used in the late 1980s by the Swedish charter airline, InterNord. InterNord only lasted a few years before the CV-990s were repossessed by American Airlines. Interestingly, the artwork is for a Boeing, not a CV-990.

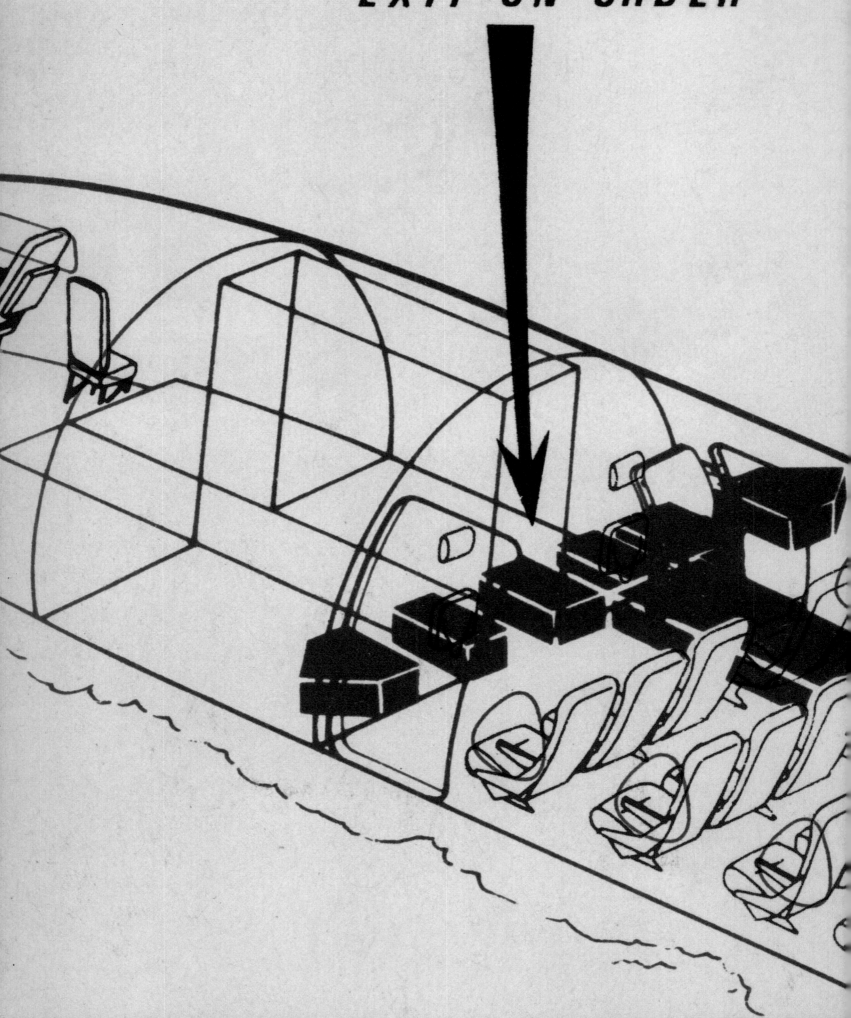

SORTIE SUR ORDRE
EXIT ON ORDER

Next-generation jets

Faster, higher, bigger. From the early 1960s onwards the goals of the aircraft industry were more ambitious than ever. The industry was expanding heavily and would do so for many years to come. The energy crisis was yet to come, and all manufacturers were extremely optimistic. The world was in their hands. And not just theirs – anybody who could spare some money and a bit of time could travel comfortably and safely just about anywhere in the world. Boeing designed and manufactured the 747 "Jumbo Jet", which is still the largest jet airplane in the world. Meanwhile, the costly but impressive Concorde project was planned in France and Britain. Yet one cannot help but feel that the first mighty steps that jet aviation took in the late 1950s are still the most important. A 707 or DC-8 looks just like any other modern plane today. Ironically, it is the Concorde which is out of step with today's environmental concerns – it proved to be too costly and inefficient when it came to fuel consumption, even if its supersonic speed is still impressive and useful for travellers who need to cross the Atlantic swiftly. But for the most part it has to be written off as a gimmick for rich people. Nevertheless, the jet airplane is still considered to be the "natural" means of transportation when travelling abroad, and few Westerners have not flown in one. Furthermore, safety in the air is greater than ever, and statistics indicate that flying is the safest way to travel, with far fewer casualties, relatively, than trains, cars and boats.

The safety cards from the next-generation jets were significantly simpler than those of their predecessors, using a more pedagogical approach to instruction design. (The exceptions are the cards used on non-Western airlines, which were still rather crude and difficult to understand.) The illustrations weren't as minimalist as those on contemporary cards, but it is clear from the graphics that safety consciousness had, nonetheless, greatly advanced.

EAS — CARAVELLE

EN TOUTES CIRCONSTANCES L'ÉQUIPAGE EST AU COURANT DES MESURES A PRENDRE ET VOUS DONNERA DES INSTRUCTIONS PRÉCISES. OBÉISSEZ PROMPTEMENT ET CALMEMENT AUX ORDRES QUI POURRONT ETRE DONNÉS. NE PERDEZ PAS VOTRE SANG-FROID.

THE CREW KNOW PERFECTLY WHAT TO DO UNDER ANY CIRCUMSTANCE AND WILL INSTRUCT YOU ACCORDINGLY. COOPERATE QUICKLY AND QUIETLY. FOLLOW THE CREW'S ORDERS. KEEP CALM.

CARAVELLE 3

CEINTURES DE SECURITE...
A SERRER LE PLUS POSSIBLE.

SAFETY BELTS...
TO BE FASTENED AS TIGHT AS POSSIBLE.

SORTIE SUR ORDRE
EXIT ON ORDER

ELOIGNEZ VOUS
KEEP AWAY

(A) OUVERTURE D'UN HUBLOT
OPENING OF A WINDOW

1° OUVREZ LE VOLET
PULL COVER OPEN

2° TIREZ LA POIGNÉE ROUGE
GRASP RED HANDLE AND PULL

3° LIBÉREZ L'ISSUE, PASSEZ-LA A L'EXTERIEUR
DISCARD ENTIRE WINDOW, THROW IT OUTWARDS

RAMPE D'ÉVACUATION
ESCAPE SLIDE

(C)
1° POUSSEZ ET BASCULEZ
PUSH OPEN HANDLE

2° OUVREZ
OPEN DOOR

(B)
1° LEVEZ
LIFT UP

2° TOURNEZ
TURN

3° SOULEVEZ
LIFT DOOR UP

EXIT

PANNEAU INDIQUANT LA POSITION DES ISSUES DE SECOURS
EMERGENCY EXITS POSITION

VOIR AU VERSO
PLEASE SEE OTHER SIDE.

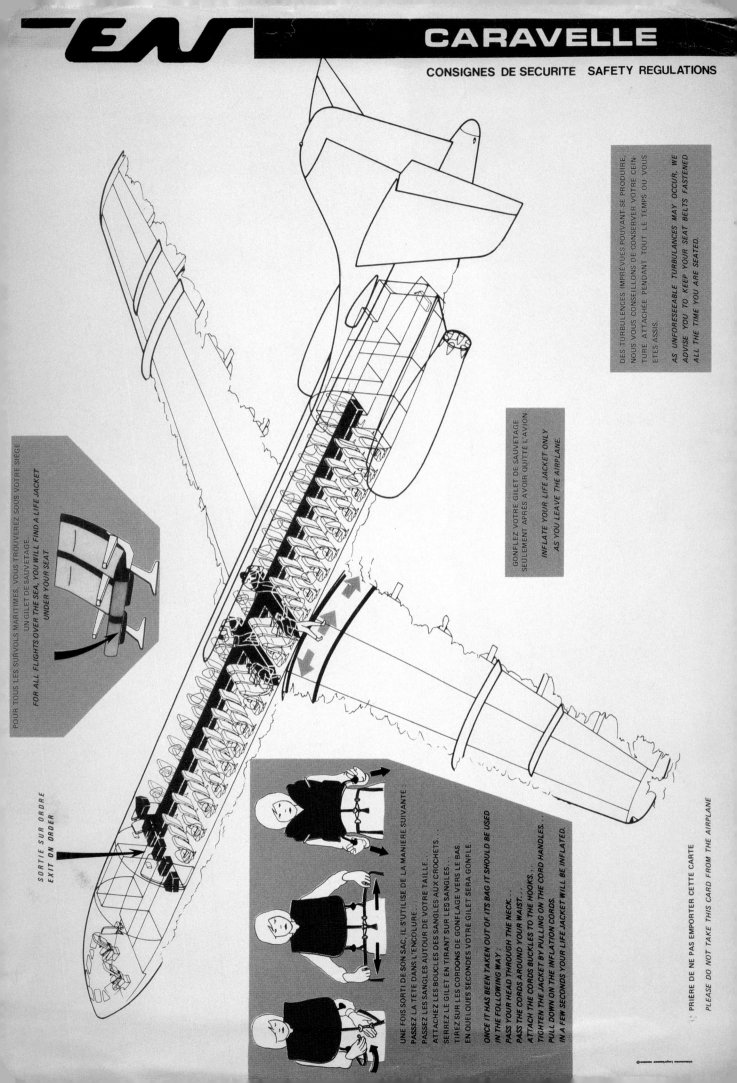

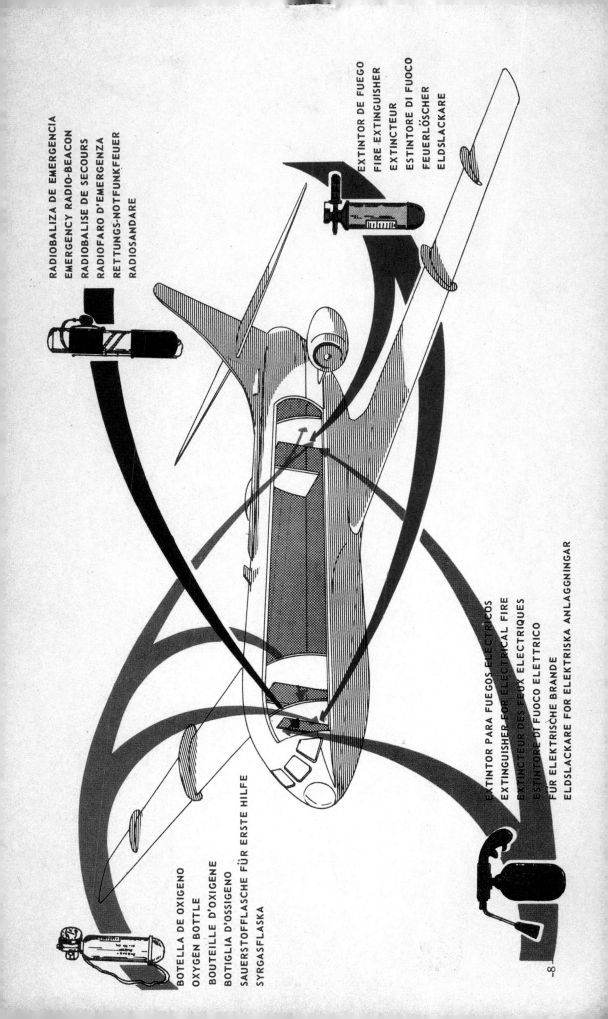

RADIOBALIZA DE EMERGENCIA
EMERGENCY RADIO-BEACON
RADIOBALISE DE SECOURS
RADIOFARO D'EMERGENZA
RETTUNGS-NOTFUNKFEUER
RADIOSANDARE

EXTINTOR DE FUEGO
FIRE EXTINGUISHER
EXTINCTEUR
ESTINTORE DI FUOCO
FEUERLÖSCHER
ELDSLACKARE

EXTINTOR PARA FUEGOS ELECTRICOS
EXTINGUISHER FOR ELECTRICAL FIRE
EXTINCTEUR DES FEUX ELECTRIQUES
ESTINTORE DI FUOCO ELETTRICO
FÜR ELEKTRISCHE BRANDE
ELDSLACKARE FOR ELEKTRISKA ANLAGGNINGAR

BOTELLA DE OXIGENO
OXYGEN BOTTLE
BOUTEILLE D'OXIGENE
BOTIGLIA D'OSSIGENO
SAUERSTOFFLASCHE FÜR ERSTE HILFE
SYRGASFLASKA

-8

IBERIA
LINEAS AEREAS DE ESPAÑA

CARAVELLE

INSTRUCCIONES DE SEGURIDAD

safety instructions   instructions de sécurité   sicherheitsinstruktionen
istruzioni di sicurezza   säkerhetsinstruktioner

✻ Le rogamos observen detenidamente las instrucciones para su seguridad como un pasatiempo más de su vuelo y por favor consulten cualquier duda que tuviesen en su interpretación. En caso de emergencia durante este vuelo se le dirá exactamente que debe hacer. No olvide que la tripulación está compuesta de expertos perfectamente adiestrados. Cumpla usted las instrucciones que reciba y sobre todo mantenga la calma. Muchas gracias.

✻ Please follow cautiously your safety instructions as an entertainment more in your flight. Do not hesitate to ask any questions you have about its interpretation. On an Emergency during this flight, you will be precisely instructed about what you should do. Do not forget the crew members are accurately trained experts, Please. follow the instructions you receive and above all keep quiet! Many Thanks!

✻ Nous prions MM. les passagers d'observer attentivement les instructions de sécurité et de les prendre comme un amusement de plus de votre vol. Nous vous prions aussi de consulter chaque doute sur leur interpretation. Au cas d'urgence durant le vol on vous dira exactement comment agir. N'oubliez pas que l'equipage est composé d'experts parfaitement instruits. Nous vous prions de suivre les instructions données et de rester calmes. Nous vous en remercions.

✻ Wir bitten unsere Passagiere freundlichst, die Sicherheitsanweisungen zu beachten und dieselben als zusätzliche Reiselektüre Ihres Flüges zu betrachten. Im Falle eines Zweifels, bitten wir Sie die Flügbegleiter zu fragen. Im Notfall werden diejenigen Ihnen genaue Anweisungen geben. Vergessen Sie bitte nicht, dass unser Flügpersonal gut trainiert ist. Bleiben Sie ruhig und folgen Sie unseren Instruktionen. Vielen Dank für Ihre Aufmerksamkeit.

✻ Vi preghiamo di voler osservare attentamente le istruzioni di sicurezza come un passatempo in piú durante il volo e di consultare il Personale di bordo in caso abbiate dei dubbi d'interpretazione. In caso d'emergenza durante il volo riceverete precise istruzioni su come comportar Vi. Non dimenticate che l'equipaggio é composto da personale esperto e perfettamente addestrato. Osservate le istruzioni che Vi saranno impartite e soprattutto mantenete la calma. Grazie.

✻ Vi ber er nograrnt läsa igenom säkerhetsdtgarderna som exrra ridsfördriv under flygturen och fraga om varje oklarhet ni har. Vid fall av olyckshändelse under den här flygturen far ni exakta order om vad som skall göras. Glöm inte att besättningen pa flyget ar sammansatt av utbilade experter. Följ instruktionerna ni far och framför allt bibehall lugn. Tack sa mycket.

Octubre 1971

CONSIGNES D'AMERRISSAGE ET D'ATTERRISSAGE FORCE

PRECAUTIONS GENERALES.

Cette notice est destinée à vous résumer les précautions prises pour votre sécurité. Cet avion possède les équipements de sécurité les plus modernes et les plus éprouvés. Chaque membre de l'équipage a été soigneusement entraîné aux manœuvres à effectuer en cas d'urgence. Faites-lui confiance et suivez ses consignes.

DISPOSITIONS PRELIMINAIRES.

1. Lorsque l'avertissement : « préparez-vous à l'amerrissage/à l'atterrissage forcé» est donné :
   1. Débarassez-vous de vos lunettes, objets pointus (crayons, clips, etc...)
   2. Desserrez votre col, enlevez votre cravate.
   3. Otez vos chaussures }
   4. Enfilez votre gilet de sauvetage } en cas d'amerrissage uniquement.
   5. Asseyez-vous et serrez votre ceinture de siège.
   6. Ne fumez pas.
II. La meilleure position à prendre vous sera expliquée par le personnel de bord; prenez cette position lorsque vous en serez avertis.

COMMENT REVETIR LE GILET DE SAUVETAGE.
1. Retirez-le de sa gaine.
2. Passez le gilet à la tête, face bleue vers vous.
3. Attachez les cordons autour de la taille SANS TROP SERRER.
4. NE GONFLEZ LE GILET QUE LORSQUE VOUS QUITTEREZ L'AVION.
5. Pour le gonflage automatique, tirez le bouton rouge d'un coup sec. Pour le regonflage, portez l'embouchure aux lèvres, appuyez et soufflez.
6. La petite lampe s'allume au contact de l'eau, lorsque la patte est arrachée.

EVACUATION DE LA CABINE.
Ne quittez votre siège que lorsque l'ordre d'évacuation sera donné, et conformez-vous aux instructions du personnel.

AANWIJZINGEN IN GEVAL VAN NOODLANDING

ALGEMENE VOORZORGSMAATREGELEN.

Deze tekst geeft een overzicht van de voorzorgsmaatregelen, getroffen met het oog op Uw veiligheid. Dit toestel is uitgerust met de modernste en meest beproefde veiligheidsinrichting. Elk bemanningslid werd nauwkeurig wat er moet gedaan worden in geval van nood. Vertrouw op hem en volg zijn bevelen op.

VOORAFGAANDE HANDELINGEN.

1. Zodra het verwittigingsbevel « Maak U klaar voor noodlanding (op zee) » weerklinkt, voert U het volgende uit :
   1. leg Uw bril en andere scherpe voorwerpen (potloden, clips, enz.) weg.
   2. maak Uw boord en Uw das los.
   3. doe Uw schoenen uit }
   4. leg uw reddingsvest om } alleen in geval van noodlanding op zee.
   5. ga zitten en maakt de riemen vast.
   6. rook niet.
II. Het personeel zal U zeggen welke houding U dient in te nemen. Voer hot uit zodra U het bevel hiertoe wordt gegeven.

HOE HET REDDINGSVEST OMLEGGEN ?
1. neem het uit de hoes.
2. trek het vest aan met de blauwe kant naar U toe.
3. maak de linten vast zonder ze te stark aan te spannen.
4. blaas het vest slechts op wanneer U het vliegtuig gaat verlaten.
5. het wordt automatisch opgeblazen door krachtig de rode knop weg te rukken. Om het opnieuw op te blazen dient men te blazen.
6. het lampje gaat branden zodra het in aanraking komt met het water wanneer het snoer is weggetrokken.

HET VERLATEN VAN DE CABINE.
Verlaat Uw zetel slechts wanneer het evacuatiebevel wordt gegeven. Gehoorzaam de instructies van het personeel.

INSTRUCTIONS FOR LANDING BY SEA OR EMERGENCY LANDING

GENERAL PRECAUTIONS.

This notice is to inform you of the precautions taken for your safety. This aircraft is provided with the most modern, fully-tested safety equipment. All members of the crew have been carefully trained in the procedure to be adopted in case of emergency. Have confidence in them and follow their instructions.

PRELIMINARY PROCEDURE.
1. On hearing the warning : « Prepare for ditching by sea/emergency landing » :
   1. Remove glasses and pointed objects (pencils, clips, etc.).
   2. Loosen collar, remove tie.
   3. Take off shoes }
   4. Put on life jacket } in case of landing by sea only.
   5. Sit down and tighten your seat belt.
   6. Do not smoke.
II. The crew will explain to you the best position to adopt; take this position when instructed.

HOW TO PUT ON YOUR LIFE JACKET.
1. Remove life jacket from case.
2. Put jacket over your head, blue side towards you.
3. Tie strings round your waist. DO NOT PULL TIGHT.
4. DO NOT INFLATE LIFE JACKET UNTIL YOU LEAVE THE AIRCRAFT.
5. To inflate automatically, pull sharply on red button. To re-inflate, put opening tot the mouth, press and blow.
6. The light will come on on contact with the water when the tab is removed.

TO EVACUATE CABIN.
Do not leave your seat until the order for evacuation is given, and follow the instructions given by the crew.

SICHERHEITSVORKEHRUNGEN FUR DEN FALL EINER NOTWASSERUNG ODER NOTLANDUNG

ALLGEMEINE SICHERHEITSMASSNAHMEN :
Durch diese Hinweise sollen Sie mit Vorkehrungen bekanntgemacht werden, die für den Notfall zu Ihrer persönlichen Sicherheit getroffen worden sind. Zunächst möchten wir feststellen, dass Ihr Flugzeug über modernste, besterprobte Unfallschutz-Ausrüstungen verfügt; ferner dass die Besatzungsmitglieder auf diesem Gebiet sorgfältig ausgebildet worden sind und sämtliche Massnahmen kennen, die gegebenenfalls durchzuführen sind. Schenken Sie ihnen Vertrauen und folgen Sie bitte ihren Anweisungen.

ERSTE SICHERHEITSMASSNAHME.
1. Nach der Ankündigung ! « Fertigmachen zur Notwasserung/Notlandung ! »
   1. Legen Sie Ihre Brille und spitzen Gegenstände (z.B. Bleistift, Ohrringe etc.,) ab.
   2. Oeffnen Sie Ihren Hemdkragen und legen Sie Ihre Krawatte ab.
   3. Ziehen Sie Ihre Schuhe aus }
   4. Legen Sie Ihre Schwimmwest an. } Nur bei vorgesehener Notwasserung.
   5. Bitte anschnallen.
   6. Bitte nicht rauchen.
II. Das Bordpersonal wird Sie von der günstigsten Körperhaltung unterrichten. Nehmen Sie diese Körperhaltung ein, sobald eine entsprechende Anweisung erfolgt.

WIE DIE SCHWIMMWESTE ANGELEGT WIRD.
1. Ziehen Sie die Schwimmweste aus ihrem Futeral.
2. Ziehen Sie dieselbe über den Kopf, wobei die blaue Seite Ihnen zugewandt sein muss.
3. Machen Sie die Schnüre in Taillenhöhe fest. (nicht zu stari anziehen !!)
4. BLASEN SIE DIE WESTE NICHT VOR VERLASSEN DES FLUGZEUGES AUF.
5. Für das automatische Aufblasen, ziehen Sie den roten Knopf mit einem kurzen Ruck auf. Bei einem späteren nochmaligen Aufblasen führen Sie das Mundstück zu den Lippen und blasen hinein.
6. Die kleine Lampe leuchtet nach Berührung mit dem Wasser auf, wenn Sie vorher die Lasche wegreissen.

VERLASSEN DER KABINE.
Verlassen Sie Ihren Platz erst, wenn die Aufforderung zum Verlassen der Kabine erfolgt ist, und halten Sie sich an die Anweisungen des Bordpersonals.

ISTRUZIONI PER L'AMMARAGGIO E L'ATTERRAGGIO FORZATI

PRECAUZIONI GENERALI.
Queste istruzioni hanno lo scopo di riassumervi le precauzioni prese per la Vostra sicurezza. Questo aereo è dotato dei più moderni e provati equipaggiamenti di sicurezza. Ciascun membro dell'equipaggio è stato accuratamente istruito sulle manovre da effettuare in caso di urgenza. Affidatevi a lui e seguite le sue istruzioni.

DISPOSIZIONI PRELIMINARI.
1. Quando viene transmesso l'avvertimento : « prepararsi all'ammaraggio o all'atterraggio forzato» :
   1. Sbarazzatevi degli occhiali e degli oggetti appuntiti (matite, spille, ecc.)
   2. Slacciatevi il colletto e levateVi la cravatta.
   3. Toglietevi le scarpe }
   4. Indossate il giubotto di salvataggio } solo in caso di ammaraggio
   5. SedeteVi e allacciate la cintura di sicurezza.
   6. Non fumare.
II. La miglior posizione da prendere Vi sarà indicata dal personale di bordo; assumete questa posizione quando sarete avvertiti.

COME INDOSSARE IL GIUBBOTTO DI SALVATAGGIO.
1. Toglietelo dalla custodia.
2. Infilatelo per la testa tenendo la parte colorata in blu verso di Voi.
3. Legate il cordone attorno alla vita SENZA STRINGERE MOLTO.
4. GONFIATE IL GIUBBOTTO SOLTANTO QUANDO USCIRETE DALL'AEREO.
5. Per il gonfiamento automatico tirate il bottone rosso con un colpo secco. Per rigonfiare portate il boccolino alle labbra e soffiatevi dentro.
6. La lampadina si accende al contatto con l'acqua appena strapperete la linguetta.

EVACUAZIONE DELLA CABINA.
Non lasciate la Vostra poltrona fino a quando non ne riceverete l'ordine e uniformateVi alle istruzioni date dal personale.

CARAVELLE VI

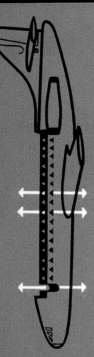

SORTIES DE SECOURS

1) Abaissez le clapet rouge marqué « EMERGENCY EXIT ».
2) Ramenez vers vous la poignée et tirez vers le bas.
3) Tirez vers vous pour faire basculer la fenêtre vers l'intérieur.

NOODUITGANGEN

1) Sla het roode luikje met het opschrift « EMERGENCY EXIT » naar beneden.
2) Haal het handvat in Uw richting en trek het naar beneden.
3) Trek naar U toe om het raam naar binnen te doen kantelen.

EMERGENCY EXITS

1) Lower red flap marked « EMERGENCY EXIT ».
2) Bring andle towards you and pull down.
3) Pull towards you to tip window inwards.

NOTAUSGÄNGE

1) Lassen Sie die rote mit « EMERGENCY EXIT » gekennzeichnete Klappe herunter.
2) Bewegen Sie den Griff auf sich.
3) Ziehen Sie auf sich zu, damit das Fenster in das Kabineninnere zurückfällt.

USCITE DI SICUREZZA

1) Abbassate il riquadro rosso su cui si trova la dicitura « EMERGENCY EXIT ».
2) Tirate verso di voi e in basso l'apposita maniglia.
3) Tirate verso di Voi per abbattere il finestrino verso l'interno.

Printed in Belgium Lint: 40M 63.

DC.6.B
DC.7.C

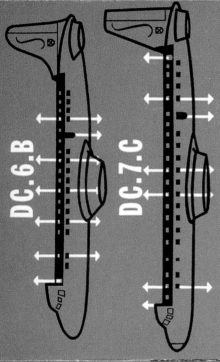

SORTIES DE SECOURS

Il faur d'abord rabattre vers l'avant le dossier du siège qui se trouve devant la fenêtre marquée «EMERGENCY EXIT ».

Ensuite :
1) Arrachez le mica qui protège la poignée marquée « EMERGENCY EXIT ».
2) Tournez cette poignée dans le sens indiqué par la flèche.
3) Poussez la fenêtre vers l'extérieur.

NOODUITGANGEN

Vooreerst de leuning van de zetel, die zich voor het « EMERGENCY EXIT »-venster bevindt, naar voren duwen.

Vervolgens :
1) Ruk het mika weg dat het handvat « EMERGENCY EXIT » dekt.
2) Draai dit handvat in de richting door de pijl aangeduid.
3) Duw het raam naar buiten.

EMERGENCY EXITS

First puch forward the back of the seat in front of the window, marked « EMERGENCY EXIT ».

Then :
1) Tear off plastic shield covering handle, marked « EMERGENCY EXIT ».
2) Turn this handle in the direction indicated by the arrow.
3) Push window outwards.

NOTAUSGÄNGE

Den Sitz vor dem Fenster mit der Aufschrift « EMERGENCY EXIT » nach vorne beugen.

1) Den Plastik-Überzug vom Griff « EMERGENCY EXIT » entfernen.
2) Den Griff in Pfeilrichtung bewegen.
3) Drücken Sie das Fenster nach aussen.

USCITE DI SICUREZZA

Abbatete in avanti la schienale della poltrona che si trova dinanzi alla finestra recante la dicitura « EMERGENCY EXIT ».

1) Rompete la mica che protegge la maniglia.
2) Girate la maniglia nel senso indicato dalla freccia ed aprite la finestra.
3) Spingete il finestrino verso l'esterno.

CONVAIR 440

SORTIES DE SECOURS

1) Enfoncez les doigts dans la plaque « EMERGENCY EXIT ».
2) Tirez vers vous et vers le bas pour faire basculer la fenêtre vers l'intérieur.

NOODUITGANGEN

1) Druk het plaatje « EMERGENCY EXIT » in.
2) Trek naar U toe en naar beneden om het raampje naar binnen te doen kantelen.

EMERGENCY EXITS

1) Insert fingers in « EMERGENCY EXIT » plaque.
2) Pull towards you and downwards to tip window inwards.

NOTAUSGÄNGE

1) Drücken Sie den mit « EMERGENCY EXIT » gekennzeichneten Deckel mit dem Finger ein.
2) Ziehen Sie das Fenster nach unten hin auf sich zu, damit es in das Kabineninnere zurückfällt.

USCITE DI SICUREZZA

1) Affondate le dita in corrispondenza della targa « EMERGENCY EXIT ».
2) Tirate verso di Voi e verso il basso per abbattere il finestrino verso l'interno.

Viscount 837

AUA
AUSTRIAN AIRLINES

Sicherheitsanweisung
Safety Instructions
Instruction de Sécurité

Caravelle VI R

AUA
AUSTRIAN AIRLINES

Sicherheitsanweisung
Safety Instructions
Instruction de Sécurité

FLY

Ghana ★ Airways

THE GREAT AIRLINE OF AFRICA

Ghana ★ Airways
Safety Information
PLEASE READ CAREFULLY

YOUR SAFETY

Your safety is our first consideration and when you fly by GHANA AIRWAYS you can always rely on every possible precaution being taken to ensure it. GHANA AIRWAYS has a very high standard of maintenance and each aircraft is subjected to a strict schedule of checks and counter-checks at regular intervals. Our flying staff are the most experienced in the world and no GHANA AIRWAYS Captain ever takes off unless and until he is satisfied the aircraft in his charge is completely fit for service.

All GHANA AIRWAYS aircraft carry enough fuel in reserve to operate far beyond their scheduled destinations. For instance, should weather conditions at the destination prevent a landing, the Captain would be able to divert to an alternative airport. Sufficient fuel would still remain for a limited period should the aircraft be prevented from landing immediately because of air traffic congestion or for any other reason. All our four-engined aircraft are capable of operating on three engines, should this be necessary; and, in certain conditions, flight can be continued on only two engines.

Each aircraft carries safety equipment for all the passengers and flying staff on board, and all GHANA AIRWAYS flying staff receive specialised training in its use and other safety procedures. The use of the life jacket will be demonstrated at the beginning of any journey over water, but this card gives further details and instructions. We hope you will find time to read what follows for although it is most unlikely to be necessary, it is important that everyone should know what he or she may be required to do should the need arise.

SEAT BELTS

Each seat on the aircraft is fitted with a belt and when the aircraft is taxying, taking off or landing, or during bumpy periods in flight, you must remain seated and fasten your seat belt when requested. On such occasions the back of your seat should be in the upright position and you should sit with your back firmly against it. Place the belt as low down as possible over the abdomen and fasten it tightly. Children too small to occupy a seat should be held in the arms of an adult but the adult's seat belt must not be round the child. If you find any difficulty, the steward or stewardess will show you what to do and help you to adjust the belt so that it fits tightly.

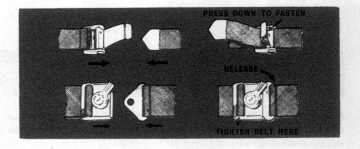

EMERGENCY EXITS

All our aircraft have emergency exits in addition to the main entry/exit doors and you can see where they are if you study the diagram. All exits are, of course, plainly marked inside the aircraft cabin. Should it be necessary to make an emergency landing, these exits may be opened by the cabin staff just before landing to enable everyone to get out as quickly as possible. The opening of these exits naturally results in a considerable amount of noise and draught and, if the landing is on the ground, dust will probably enter the cabin but need not cause alarm.

VC10

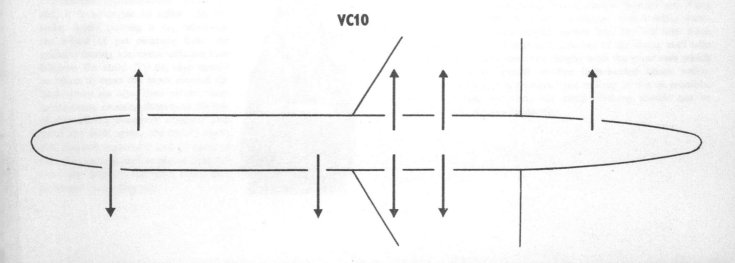

✈BOAC Safety Instructions
Consignes de Sécurité
Instrucciones de Seguridad

STANDARD VC10

Seat belts   Ceintures   Cinturones de asiento

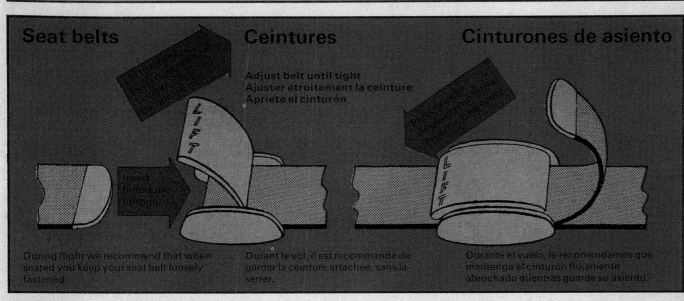

Adjust belt until tight
Ajuster étroitement la ceinture
Apriete el cinturón

Insert
Introduire
Introduzca

During flight we recommend that when seated you keep your seat belt loosely fastened.

Durant le vol, il est recommandé de garder la ceinture attachée, sans la serrer.

Durante el vuelo, le recomendamos que mantenga el cinturón flojamente abrochado mientras guarde su asiento.

Oxygen   Oxygène   Oxígeno

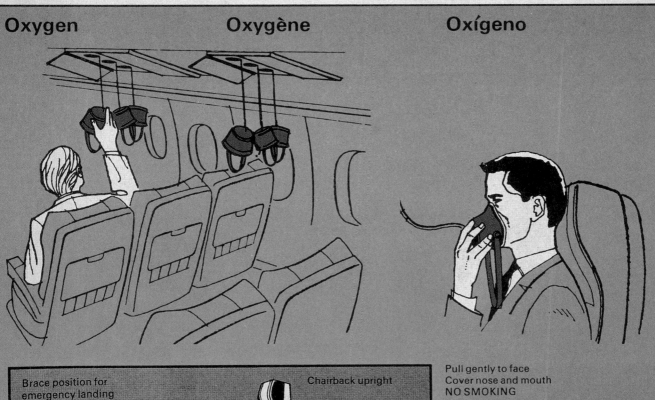

Brace position for emergency landing

Position à adopter en cas d'atterrissage forcé

Posición para aterrizaje de emergencia

Chairback upright

Dossier du fauteuil relevé

Respaldo del asiento derecho

Pull gently to face
Cover nose and mouth
NO SMOKING

Tirer doucement vers le visage
Couvrir le nez et la bouche
INTERDICTION DE FUMER

Lléveselo suavemente hacia la cara
Cubra naríz y boca
PROHIBIDO FUMAR

⤐ BOAC Safety Instructions
Consignes de Sécurité
Instrucciones de Seguridad

STANDARD VC10

Your lifejacket
is under your seat
Do not inflate in cabin

Votre gilet de sauvetage
se trouve sous le siège
Ne pas gonfler dans la cabine

Su salvavidas
está debajo del asiento
No lo infle dentro del avión

1st Class

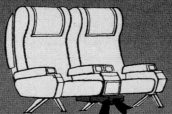

Economy Class

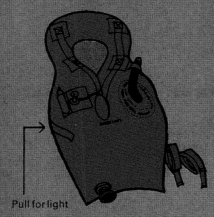

Pull for light

Tirer pour l'allumage

Tire para encender la luz

Pass over your head, cross tapes at back

Enfiler par la tête et croiser les sangles dans le dos

Páseselo por la cabeza. Lleve las cintas alrededor del cuerpo, cruzándolas en la espalda

Tie securely at front

Nouer solidement devant

Atelas bien sobre la cintura al frente

To inflate—pull red knob smartly down. If necessary, top-up using mouth piece

Gonflage—tirer vivement vers le bas le bouton rouge. Si nécessaire, achever de gonfler avec la valve à bouche

Para inflar—jale con fuerza la perilla roja hacia abajo. Si es necesario inflar más, sople en la boquilla

Life cots for infants
Berceaux de sauvetage pour bébés
Cunas salvavidas para bebés

Wrap infant in blanket
Fix straps diagonally
Fix hood just before leaving aircraft

Envelopper l'enfant dans une couverture
Mettre les sangles en diagonale
Ne fixer la capote qu'au moment de l'évacuation de l'appareil

Envuelva al bebé en le manta
Sujete las cintas diagonalmente
Cubra con el capuchón justo en el momento de abandonar el avión

Lifejackets for children
Gilets de sauvetage pour enfants
Salvavidas para niños

Inflate
Pass over head
Cross tapes above hips and over buoyancy chamber
Tie at back

Gonfler d'abord
Enfiler par la tête
Croiser les sangles au-dessus des hanches sur le gilet
Nouer dans le dos

Infle el salvavidas
Páseselo por la cabeza
Pase las cintas encima de las caderas, crúcelas sobre la cámara inflada
Atelas a la espalda

Liferafts
Canots de sauvetage
Botes salvavidas

Sufficient liferafts are carried to accommodate all passengers and crew

Des canots de sauvetage suffisamment vastes pour contenir tous les passagers et l'équipage sont transportés à bord de l'appareil

Hay a bordo botes salvavidas suficientes para todo el pasaje y la tripulación

Printed in Great Britain

Seat belt
No Smoking during Take-off and Landing

أحزمة المقاعد •
ممنوع التدخين أثناء
الاقلاع والهبوط •

Oxygen
No Smoking

اوكسجين
ممنوع التدخين

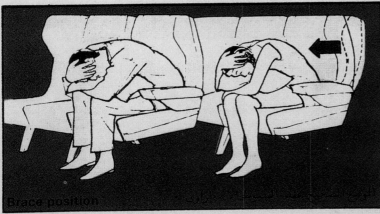

Brace position

Your lifejacket
Do not inflate inside the aircraft

لا تنفخ سترة النجاة داخل الطائرة ·
بعد الخروج من الطائرة اسحب الزر الأحمر
فتنتفخ السترة تلقائيا ·

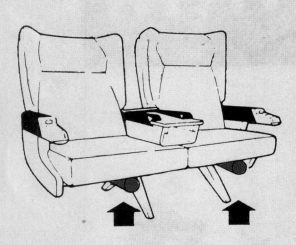

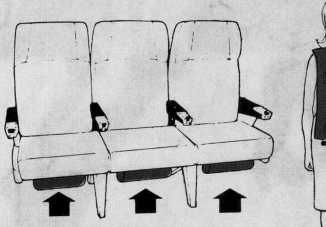

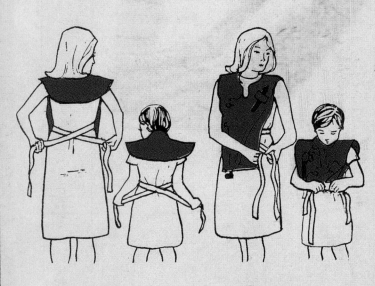

BAC 1-11

Safety instructions

Instructions de sécurité

Sicherheits-Instruktionen

Istruzioni di sicurezza

Instrucciones de seguridad

Instruções de segurança

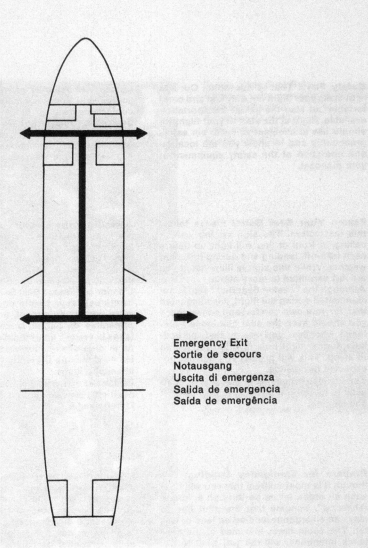

Emergency Exit
Sortie de secours
Notausgang
Uscita di emergenza
Salida de emergencia
Saída de emergência

LIFE JACKETS

When instructed by crew put on life jacket. Do not inflate in cabins. To put on life jacket, pull over head, pass tapes round waist, and then cross them to bring to front. Tie tapes in secure knot under jacket in front.

GILETS DE SAUVETAGE

Les instructions données, utiliser le gilet de sauvetage. Ne pas le gonfler dans la caline. Pour l'utiliser, le passer par la tëte, attacher les boucles autour de la taille et les passer devant. Nouer les cordons au-dessous bu gilet devant.

LIFE JACKET LAYOUT

1. Mouth inflation tube used only when automatic device fails or for "topping up"
2. Tie tapes.
3. Automatic inflation knob. Pull down smartly to inflate jacket.
4. Whistle for attracting attention in the dark.
5. Light for attracting attention in the dark.

ETUDE DU GILET DE SAUVETAGE

1) Le gonflage par la bouche doit se faire seu-lement quand le système automatique fait défaut.
2) Nouer les rubans
3) Règlage automtique du gonflant
4) Siffler pour attirer votre attention dans l'obscurité
5) Allumer pour attirer l'attention dans l'obscurité

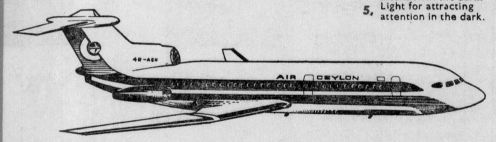

SEAT BELTS

The illuminated signs must be obeyed. From experience we recommend that you keep your seat belt on and comfortably fastened when in your seat to avoid being disturbed in the event of turbulence being encountered.

EMERGENCY LANDING

In the event of an emergency landing:
1. Cease smoking.
2. Fasten seat belt.
3. Seat upright.
4. Place pillow in lap and rest head on pillow with the other arm around the top of head.
5. Bend forward with one arm across knees.
6. Brace for impact on landing and remain braced until the aircraft finally comes to rest.

Life jackets are under your seat. Loosen collar and tie, remove spectacles, false teeth, high heeled shoes and any other sharp or breakable items. Get in position for impact as described in Emergency Landing, on instruction from crew.

LIFE JACKETS FOR CHILDREN

Cross the tapes round the back and above hips before returning them to the front. Cross them over the top and finally tie the ends across the child's back.

CEINTURE

Les panneaux de lumière doivent ëtre respectés. De l'expérience, nous vous recommandons de conserver la ceinture attachée mais non serrée. Vous serez ainsi protégé des turbulences imprévues.

ATTERRISSAGE FORCE

Dans le cas d'un atterrissage forcé:
1) Cesser de fumer
2) Attacher la ceinture
3) Redresser le dossier de votre siège
4) Placer sur les genoux un coussin et y reposant votre tëte et en plaçant l'autre bras tout autour de la tëte.
5) Se courber en avant ayant un bras autour des genoux.
6) Prendre la position d'impact jusqu'à ce que l'avion s'arrête.

Vos gilets de sauvetage sont logés sous vos sièges. Défaire votre col et cravate, ôter des verres, la denture, les chaussures haut-talons ou tout autre instrument pointu ou fragile. Prendre la position d'impact comme décrit au moment d'atterrissage forcé sur instruction de l'équipage.

GILETS DE SAUVETAGE POUR ENFANTS

Attacher les rubans en croix au-dessus des hanches au dos avant. de les passer en avant. Retirer les en haut et finalement nouer les bouts au dos de l'enfant.

හදිසියෙන් නික්මීම

සියලුම නික්මෙන දෙරටු පැහැදිලිව සළකුණු කොට ඇත. ඒවා ඇතුළත ඇරේ. ගුවන් සේවක පිරිස විසින් එම දෙරටු අර දෙනු ලැබේ.

යුතුකුඩුන් නික්මීම යාත්‍රාව තතර කරනතුරුම දෙරුමක් දරාගැනීමේ සුදානමින් ඔබ පිරිස යුතුය ගැස්සීම එක වරකට වඩා සිදුවිය හැකි බැවින්. අසුන පටි ඉවත් කළ යුත්තේ යානාව තතර කළ පසුවය. යානයෙන් පිටත දී ඇකුරටුවේ රතු මුර්ච්චිය පහතට ඇදීමෙන් ඉය පුමංගන්න පුරණ ලෙස පුඹා ගැනීමට මුඛ නලය පාවිච්චි කරන්න. ඉය උඩින් දීර්ය ලෙස පියයර කිරීමට මත්තෙන් මේ ජීවිත ආරක්ෂක ඇකුටටු පාවිච්චිය පිළිබඳ ආදර්ශනයක් දීම සේවක පිරිස විසින් සිදු කෙරෙනු ඇත.

ගිලීගෙන කවුළු යාත්‍රයේ දෙරටු ඇත්තේ පොළවට තරමක් උඩින් බැවින් මගීන්ට ගිලීම සඳහා මෙම කවුළු පහතින් ඇත්තේය. කාන්තාවෝ ඔවුන්ගේ අඩි උස සපත්තු ඉවත් කළ යුතුය. කවුළුවේ පැත්ත අල්ලා ගත යුතු නැති අතර එයට පැනීමෙන් වැළකිය යුතුය. මෙසේ ගිලීමෙන් පසු කවුළුවෙන් හා යානයෙන් ඈත් වන්න.

ජීවිත ආරක්ෂක තොට්ටි ළදරුවන්ගේ සහ ළමයින්ගේ ආරක්ෂාව සඳහා මේවා සපයනු ලැබේ අරක්ෂා සහිතව පාවෙන එති වියන අර්ධ වශයෙන් විනිවිද පෙනේ. අඩියෙහි සුළං පිරි ඇත. මේ සියල්ලෙන් සහතික වන්නේ ආරක්ෂාවයි.

පාවිච්චිය: තොට්ටිය අසුරණයෙන් එළියට ගන්න. පිඹීම සඳහා රතු උපකරණ දෙරුවා දෙරුව තොට්ටිල්ලේ තබා පැබ්රික් පටි වලින් බඳින්න. එකක් පපුව හරහාත් අනික බඩ හරහාත් තදකරන්න. වියන එසවිය යුත්තේ යානයෙන් පිටත යැවෙන ආසාන්නයේ දී ය.

ඔක්සිජන් උපකරණ වේදන අවශ්‍යාවන් සඳහා ඔක්සිජන් ඇත. කුටිනය තුල පිඩනය මද කිරීම අවශ්‍ය වුවහොත් – එවැනි අවස්ථාවකදී මැ‍ජයකුට නිරායාසයෙන් ඔක්සිජන් ලබා ගත හැක්කේය ඔබ වෙත එන කෝප්පයක හැඩ ඇති ආවරණය මුහුණ මත තබා සාමාන්‍ය පිළිවෙලට හුස්ම ගැනීමේ ඔබ කළයුත්තේ.

(தமிழ்)

குழந்தைகளுக்குரிய உயிர்காப்பு மேலுடைகள்: நாடாக்களை முதுகைச் சுற்றியும், இடுப்புக்கு மேலாகவும் வரிந்து, முன்புறமாகக் கொண்டு வரவும் மேற்புறம் குறுக்குப் பக்கமாக எடுத்து கடைசியில் நாடாவின் அந்தங்களை குழந்தையின் முதுகுப் புறம் கொண்டு வந்து கட்டவும்.

உங்கள் பாதுகாப்பு: இந்த விமானத்தில் உங்கள் பாதுகாப்புக்காக மேற்கொள்ளப்பட்டிருக்கும் முன்னேற்பாடுகளையும் வசதிகளையும் நீங்கள் அறிந்து கொள்ள வேண்டுமென்பது சட்ட விதி. ஆகவே இதனைக் கவனமாகப் படித்து, அவசியமேற்பட்டால் விமான ஊழியர் சொல்படி அமைந்து நடந்து அவர்களுக்கு ஒத்துழைக்கவும்.

அபாய வேளையில் வெளியேறுதற்குரிய வாயில்கள்: வெளி வழிகள் யாவும் தெளிவாகக் குறிக்கப்பட்டுள்ளன. வெளி வழி யன்னல்கள் உட்பக்கமாகத் திறக்கப்படுவன. அவசியம் நேரும் போது விமான ஊழியர் அவற்றைத் திறந்து விடுவர்.

விமானத்திலிருந்து வெளியேறுதல்: விமானத்தில் ஒரு முறைக்குப் புலமுறை குலுக்கம் ஏற்படலாமாகையால் அது நிலையாக நிற்கும் வரை அதிர்ச்சியை எதிர்பார்த்துத் தயாராக இருக்கவும். நிலையாக நிற்கும் முன் ஆசனப் பட்டிகளைத் தளர்த்தலாகாது. இதன் பிறகு, விமானத்திலிருந்து எப்படி வெளியேறுவதென்று விமான ஊழியர் உங்களுக்கு விளக்குவார். விமானத்துக்கு வெளியே வந்ததும், உயிர் காப்பு மேலுடையின் அடியில் உள்ள குமிழை கச்சிதமாகக் கீழே இழுத்துக் காற்றேற்றச் செய்யவும். காற்று இறுக்கமாக நிரம்புதற்கு வாய்க் குழாயைப் பயன்படுத்தலவும். நீர்ப் பரப்பின் மீதாக நெடும் பயணம் செய்யு முன், உயிர்காப்பு மேலுடையை அணியும் விதம் பற்றி விமான ஊழியர் உங்களுக்கு விளக்குவார்.

தப்பிச் செல்வதற்குரிய சாய்கலங்கள்: விமானத்தின் கதவுகளுக்கும் தரைக்குமிடையே உயரம் அதிகமாக இருந்தால், கீழே இறங்குவதற்கென சாய்கலங்கள் வழங்கப்படும். பிரயாணிகள் இவற்றில் அமர்ந்து சருக்கிக் கீழே வரலாம். பெண்மணிகள் இவற்றில் அமர்ந்து செல்லும்போது காலணிகளைக் கழற்றிக் கொள்ள வேண்டும். சாய்கலத்தின் கரைப் பக்கத்தில் தங்க வேண்டாம். சாய் கலத்துள் பாயவும் வேண்டாம். வெளியேறியபின் சாய்கலம், விமானம் ஆகியவற்றுக்கு அப்பால் செல்லவும்.

உயிர்காப்புத் தொட்டில்கள்: குழந்தைகள், சிறுவர்களின் பாதுகாப்புக்கென உயிர்காப்புத் தொட்டில்கள் உண்டு. இவை பத்திரமாக மிதப்பவை. அரைக்கரைவாசி வெளிக்காட்டக் கூடிய கூடாரமும் காப்பிட்ட அடித்தளமும் பாதுகாப்பின் உறுதிப்படுத்துகின்றன. உபயோகிக்கும் முறை: தொட்டிக் கலத்திலிருந்து எடுக்கவும். காற்றூதுதற்கு சிவப்பு நிறக் கருவால் இழுக்கவும். குழந்தை தொட்டிலிட்டு, அதில் உள்ள துணிப் பட்டியால் கட்டவும். ஒரு கூறு பட்டியைக் மார்பில் குறுக்காகவும் மற்றக் கூறினைக் கால்களுக்குக் குறுக்காகவும் கட்டவும். விமானத்திலிருந்து வெளியேறும் தருணத்தில் கூடாரத்தை நிமிர்த்தி விடவும்.

பிராண வாயுக் கருவி: வைத்திய தேவைகளுக்கென ஒக்ஸிஜன் உண்டு. கபினுடைய அழுத்தத்தைக் குறைக்க வேண்டி நேர்ந்தால் ஒவ்வொரு பிரயாணிக்கும் தானகவே ஒக்ஸிஜன் இடைப்பதற்கு ஏற்பாடு செய்யப்படும். சிரசுக்கு மேலேயிருக்கும் சேகரக் கலத்திலிருந்து கிண்ணம் போன்ற முகமூடிகள் கீழே விழும். நீங்கள் அந்த முகமூடியை உங்கள் முகத்துக்கு நேராகப் பிடித்து வழக்கம்போலச் சுவாசித்தால் சரி.

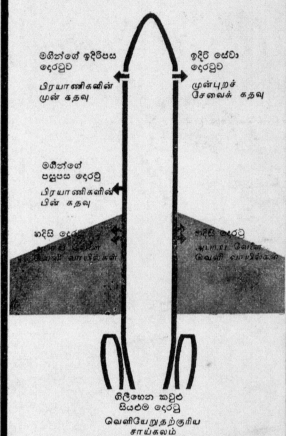

மகீன்ගே இදිரිපස දෙරටුව / இடிரி சேவா தெரටுவ
பிரயாணிகளின் முன் கதவு / முன்புறச் சேவைக் கதவு

மகீன்ගே පසුපස දෙරටුව / பிரயாணிகளின் பின் கதவு

ஹදிசி தெரடுව / ஹදிசி தெரடுව

ගිලීහෙන කවුළු සියඅம දෙරටු
வெளியேறுதற்குரிய சாய்கலம் எல்லாக் கதவுகளிலும் உண்டு.

CYPRUS AIRWAYS

Safety on board
'Ασφάλεια ἐπὶ ἀεροπλάνου
Sicherheit an bord

TRIDENT TWO

Safety Instructions

Your safety in our care is our first concern. Flying with a modern airline is safe but it is prudent that you should know what to do in any emergency, and we ask you to read this card carefully.

In case of emergency, please obey implicitly the instructions of the crew, as they will often be able to direct you to a door or emergency exit which is nearer to your seat than the door by which you entered the aircraft.

'Οδηγίες ἀσφαλείας

'Η ἀσφάλειά σας στά χέρια μας εἶναι ἡ σπουδαιότερη φροντίδα μας. Ταξιδεύοντας μὲ μιά σύγχρονη ἀεροπορικὴ ἑταιρεία εἶναι, βέβαια, ἀκίνδυνο, μὰ εἶναι φρόνιμο νὰ ξέρετε τί πρέπει νὰ κάνετε σὲ μιά περίπτωση ἐπειγούσης ἀνάγκης. Σᾶς παρακαλοῦμε, λοιπόν, νὰ διαβάσετε προσεχτικὰ τίς ὁδηγίες πού παραθέτουμε πιό κάτω.

Σὲ περίπτωση ἐπειγούσης ἀνάγκης σᾶς παρακαλοῦμε ν' ἀκολουθῆτε αὐστηρὰ τὶς ὁδηγίες τοῦ πληρώματος, γιατί αὐτοί μποροῦν πιό εὔκολα νὰ σᾶς ὁδηγήσουν σὲ μιά πόρτα ἤ ἄλλη ἔξοδο κινδύνου, πού εἶναι πιό κοντὰ στὸ κάθισμά σας ἀπό ἐκείνη ἀπ' τὴν ὁποία εἴχατε μπῆ στ' ἀεροπλάνο.

Anweisungen für das Verhalten in Notfällen

Während Sie sich in unserer Obhut befinden, ist Ihre Sicherheit unser oberstes Gebot. Moderne Flugzeuge sind sicher, aber trotzdem sollten Sie wissen, wie man sich im Notfall verhält. Darum bitten wir Sie, diesen Abschnitt über Sicherheit gut durchzulesen.

Bei Gefahr befolgen Sie bitte genau die Anweisungen der Besatzung, da sie Ihnen oft einen Notausgang zeigen kann, der Ihrem Sitz näher liegt als die Tür, durch die Sie das Flugzeug betraten.

Escape Slides

Escape slides are available by the main doors to enable passengers to reach the ground without the use of airport steps. If necessary, the operation will be supervised by the crew.

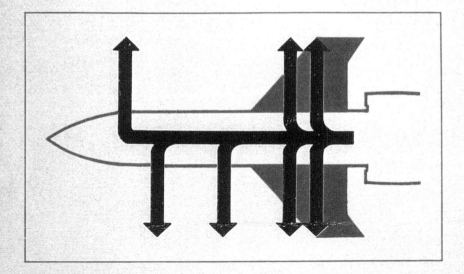

'Ολισθητῆρες ἐξόδου

Εἰδικοί ὀλισθητῆρες γιά τὴν ἔξοδο ἀπό τ' ἀεροπλάνο τοποθετοῦνται σὲ περίπτωση ἐπειγούσης ἀνάγκης στίς κύριες πόρτες τοῦ ἀεροπλάνου γιά νά διευκολύνουν τούς ἐπιβάτες νὰ φθάσουν στὸ ἔδαφος χωρὶς νά χρησιμοποιήσουν τὶς σκάλες τοῦ ἀεροδρομίου. ''Αν ὑπάρξη τέτοια ἀνάγκη ἡ χρησιμοποίηση τῶν ὀλισθητήρων θὰ γίνη ὑπό τὴν ἄγρυπνη παρακολούθηση τῶν μελῶν τοῦ πληρώματος.

Notrutsche

Die Passagier-Notrutschen befinden sich bei den Hauptausgängen, mit deren Hilfe Sie das Flugzeug ohne Treppe verlassen können. Sollte die Rutsche gebraucht werden, erfolgt dies unter Anleitung der Besatzung.

Emergency Landing Instructions

In the event of an emergency landing, the Captain will first of all announce 'Prepare for an emergency landing'. In this event please keep calm and carry out the following instructions.

1. Loosen neck wear, remove glasses, dentures and high-heeled shoes and empty pockets of sharp objects. Extinguish all cigarettes and do not use lighters or matches.

2. Ensure your seat back is in the vertical position and fasten your seat belt.

'Οδηγίες γιά καταναγκαστικὴ προσγείωση

Σὲ περίπτωση πού θά γίνη καταναγκαστικὴ προσγείωση ὁ κυβερνήτης πρῶτα-πρῶτα ·θ' ἀνακοινώση «Ἑτοιμασθῆτε γιά καταναγκαστικὴ προσγείωση». Σὲ μιά τέτοια περίπτωση σᾶς παρακαλοῦμε νὰ μείνετε ἤρεμοι καὶ νὰ ἐκτελέσετε τὶς ἀκόλουθες ὁδηγίες:

1. Χαλαρῶστε τὸν κολλάρο καὶ τὴ γραβάτα σας, βγάλτε τὰ γυαλιά, τεχνητὲς ὀδοντοστοιχίες καὶ παπούτσια μὲ ψηλὰ τακούνια κι' ἀδειάστε τὶς τσέπες σας ἀπό μυτερά καὶ κοφτερὰ ἀντικείμενα.

Σβῦστε τὰ τσιγάρα σας καὶ μή χρησιμοποιῆτε ἀναπτῆρες ἤ σπίρτα.

Anweisungen für den Fall einer Notlandung

Wenn eine Notlandung bevorsteht, hören Sie zunächst die Durchsage des Kapitäns: 'Prepare for an Emergency Landing'. Bewahren Sie bitte Ruhe und verhalten Sie sich wie folgt:

1. Um den Hals getragene Kleidungsstücke lösen, Augengläser, künstliches Gebiss und Schuhe mit hohen Absätzen ablegen und scharfe Gegenstände aus den Taschen nehmen. Zigarette löschen. Feuerzeug und Streichhölzer nicht benutzen.

CYPRUS AIRWAYS

Safety on board
'Ασφάλεια ἐπί ἀεροπλάνου
Sicherheit an bord

TRIDENT TWO

Emergency Exits ῎Εξοδοι κινδύνου Notausgange

Doors Πόρτες Türen Windows Παράθυρα Fenster

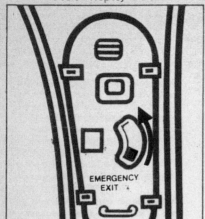

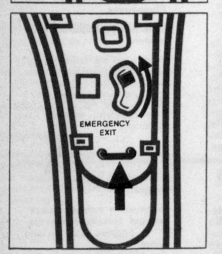

Oxygen Masks
Προσωπίδες ὀξυγόνου
Sauerstoff Gerät

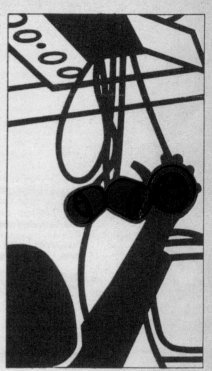

Oxygen Masks

If an oxygen supply becomes necessary, simple cup-shaped masks will drop out from overhead stowages. Masks must be pulled down fully to make the supply of oxygen available.
Hold masks firmly over the nose and mouth and continue to breathe normally.
Please ensure, your cigarette is extinguished before using the Oxygen mask.

Προσωπίδες ὀξυγόνου

῎Αν χρειασθῆ νά γίνη χρήση ὀξυγόνου, ἁπλές προσωπίδες ὀξυγόνου θά βρεθοῦν αὐτόματα μπροστά σας στή θέση σας, μιά γιά κάθε ἐπιβάτη. Τραβήξατε τήν καλά κάτω πρός τό μέρος σας γιά νά μπορῆ νά ἐλευθερωθῆ τό ὀξυγόνο. Κρατῆστε τήν καλά μπροστά στή μύτη καί τό στόμα σας καί συνεχίστε ν' ἀναπνέετε κανονικά.
Παρακαλοῦμε προτοῦ χρησιμοποιήσετε τήν προσωπίδα ὀξυγόνου βεβαιωθῆτε ὅτι ἔχετε σβύσει τό τσιγάρο σας.

Sauerstoff Gerät

Sollte der Sauerstoff in der Kabine auf einen Tiefstand sinken, fällt automatisch eine becherförmige Maske vom oberen Ablagebord. Diese Masken müssen ganz heruntergezogen werden, bevor der Sauerstoff herausströmt. Halten Sie die Maske fest auf Nase und Mund gepresst und atmen Sie normal weiter.
Bitte überzeugen Sie sich, ob Ihre Zigarette ausgelöscht ist, vor der Benutzung Ihrer Maske.

PRINTED BY ZAVALLIS PRESS - NICOSIA

IRAN AIR
The Airline of the
ISLAMIC REPUBLIC OF IRAN

727_200 SAFETY INSTRUCTIONS

* EXIT DOOR

EXIT

OPEN

PULL TO INFLATE

* EXIT WINDOW

EXIT

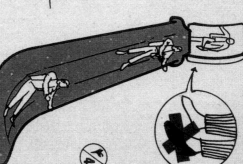

Please don't take this card away from Aircraft

Form No. 920-2-5

OXYGEN MASK

مطلب آکسیژن

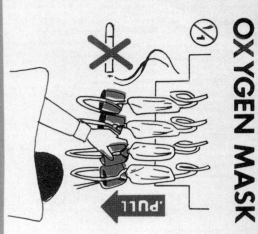

PULL

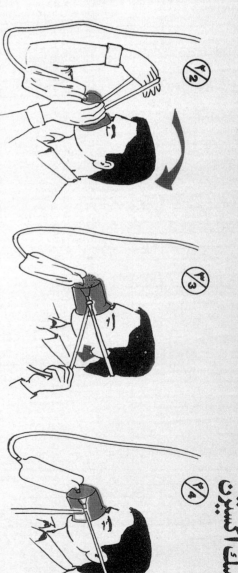

BRACING POSITION FOR EMERGENCY LANDING

آماده شدن برای نشست اضطراری

LIFE JACKET

BOEING 727

100   200

LLOYD AEREO BOLIVIANO S.A.

INSTRUCCIONES PARA SU SEGURIDAD
INSTRUCTIONS FOR YOUR SAFETY
INSTRUÇÕES PARA SUA SEGURANÇA

OXIGENO
OXYGEN

ASIENTOS
— Durante el despegue y aterrizaje, usted debe mantener el respaldo de su asiento en posición vertical.
SEATS
— During take off and landing, you must keep your seat back in vertical position.

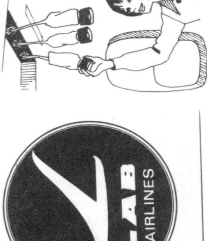

LAB
AIRLINES

SALIDAS DE EMERGENCIA
EMERGENCY EXITS

727-200

Tenga la bondad de no llevarse esta tarjeta

Please do not remove this card from the plane

BOEING 737

CONSIGNES DE SÉCURITÉ

AIR MADAGASCAR

SAFETY INSTRUCTIONS
SICHERHEITS VORSCHRIFTEN
CONSIGNAS DE SECURIDAS

DECOLLAGE ET ATTERRISSAGE - AT TAKE-OFF AND LANDING
VOR START UND LANDUNG - DURANTE EL DESPEGUE Y EL ATERRIZAJE

Des turbulences imprévues pouvant se produire, nous vous conseillons de conserver votre ceinture attachée pendant tout le temps où vous êtes assis

As unforeseeable turbulances may occur, we advise you to keep your seat belts fastened all the time you are seated.

Da unvorhergesehene Wirbel entstehen können, raten wir Ihnen, Ihren Gürtel während der Zeit, in der Sie sitzen, festgeschnallt zu behalten.

Como se pueden producir turbulencias atmosféricas imprevistas le aconsejamos que mantenga abrochado su cinturón durante todo el tiempo que permanezca sentado.

ATTACHER VOS CEINTURES	NE PAS FUMER
FASTEN SEAT BELT	NO SMOKING

AIR MADAGASCAR

BOEING 737

CONSIGNES DE SÉCURITÉ

AIR MADAGASCAR

SAFETY INSTRUCTIONS
SICHERHEITS VORSCHRIFTEN
CONSIGNAS DE SECURIDAS

OXYGENE / OXYGEN / SAUERSTOFF / OXIGENO

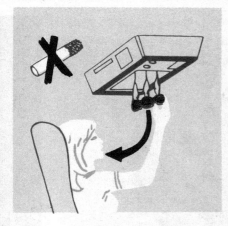
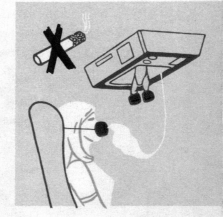

GILET DE SAUVETAGE / LIFE JACKET / RETTUNGSWESTE / CHALECO SALVAVIDAS

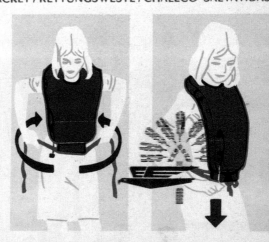

ne gonflez votre gilet qu'après en avoir reçu l'ordre
wait for crew order to inflate your jacket
Schwimmweste erst dann aufblasen, wenn Sie dazu aufgefordert werden
no infle su chaleco antes de recibir la orden correspondiente

Page 125. EAS, Caravelle. This card was used in the early to mid-1970s.

Page 127. Iberia, Caravelle. Dating from October 1971, this card was the last version before the aircraft was retired.

Page 129. Sabena, Convair 440, Douglas DC-6, DC-7 and Caravelle. A fleet card from 1963.

Page 131. Austrian Airlines, Caravelle. This card is from the early 1960s. Several different versions of this card exist, with varying covers and logo styles, although they have the same reference number and date.

Page 133. Ghana Airways, Douglas VC-10. This card is similar in format to the one used by B.O.A.C. at the time, since B.O.A.C. did the technical work for Ghana Airways at Heathrow Airport in London. It dates from the late 1970s.

Page 135. B.O.A.C., Douglas VC-10. This card is from the late 1960s.

Page 137. Gulf Air, Douglas VC-10. This card is also similar to those used by B.O.A.C. during the same period. Gulf Air introduced its own international VC-10 service in the early 1970s. Previously this service was operated by B.O.A.C., with B.O.A.C. aircraft carrying "Gulf Air" stickers, but with B.O.A.C. crews.

Page 139. Swissair, BAC 1-11. A card from the late 1960s. The aircraft was leased from the U.K. for additional summer capacity. It was painted in full Swissair colours, but was operated by British crews.

Page 141. Air Ceylon, Trident. This card dates from the early 1980s.

Page 143. Cyprus Airways, Trident. This card is roughly based on the BEA cards of the same period. Cyprus Airways was associated with BEA for the purposes of management and technical services at the time.

Page 145. Iran Air, Boeing 727-200. The 727-100 card was changed to 727-200. This card is still in use. Note the sticker to correct the aircraft specification.

Page 147. Lloyd Aereo Boliviano, Boeing 727-100 and 727-200. This card is from the mid-1970s.

Page 149. Air Madagascar, Boeing 737. This card is from the early 1980s.

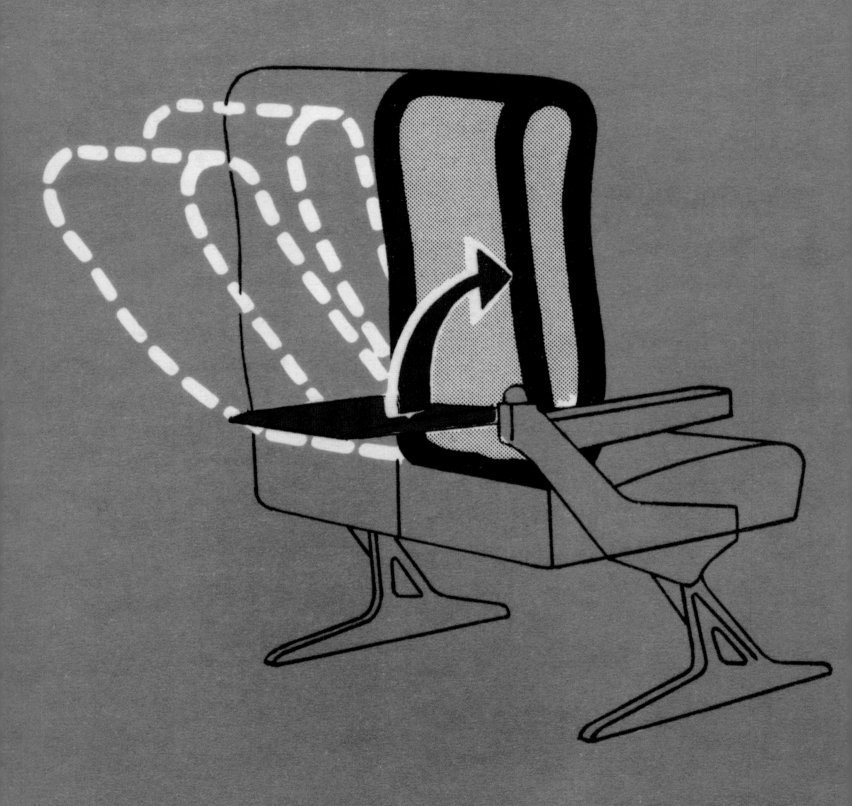

The Concorde

The Concorde marked a milestone in aviation history, as did the early cards from the aircraft. They were very beautiful pieces of work, meticulously illustrated and printed on high-quality paper. But times have changed, and today's Concorde cards are no different from those of other airlines, when it comes to production values.

Towards the end of the 1950s, the idea of France and Britain working together on a new airplane project took shape. Even though both countries had made their own passenger jets – the Caravelle and the Comet – it became obvious that a truly advanced project might be achieved by the two nations' industries co-operating. The U.S. airliner industry had been very successful, with Boeing and Douglas selling their 707s and DC-8s to all of the world's major airlines, while the Comet and Caravelle were struggling.

In 1962, French president Charles de Gaulle made an official request for Britain and France to collaborate on the building of a civil aircraft which concentrated on speed rather than increased passenger capacity, adding that he would like this aircraft to fly at supersonic speed. By the end of the year, officials on both sides had signed an agreement. It stipulated that Britain and France "must in all aspects of the project make an equal contribution, regarding both the costs to be taken on and the work to be carried out, and to share equally proceeds from sales". The building of this aircraft was entrusted to four companies: the British Aircraft Corporation and Sud Aviation were to be responsible for building the airframe, while the Olympus 593 jet engines would be manufactured by Bristol Siddeley of Britain and SNECMA of France. Later Rolls-Royce took over the British engine-plant.

In 1964, Britain's new Labour government announced the withdrawal from the Concorde project. In January 1965, they had a change of heart and the project continued. But not without difficulties.

The language barrier proved to be difficult; few of the French, except for the sales people, spoke English, and the Britons' knowledge of French was often quite limited.

Many meetings were held in both languages, and much time was wasted in interpreting. The Concorde project took time and money, but interest was, nevertheless, tremendous. By 1967, 74 sales options from 16 airlines had dropped in, although the option list for the American Supersonic project – which was discontinued in 1971 – was rumoured to be twice as long. At the end of 1967, the first prototype, the French Concorde 001, was completed. It was not ready to fly, however, and the Soviet Tupolev 144, considered to be a rip-off of the Concorde, beat the aircraft to be the first supersonic passenger airplane in the air, in December 1968. The Concorde did not make it off the ground until March 1969.

The testing continued, and the Concorde prototypes soon reached Mach 2, twice the speed of sound. But at the beginning of 1973, the project experienced a major setback when TWA and Pan Am announced that they would not take up their options to buy the Concorde. The two airlines were, at this time, the biggest long-haul operators in the world, and their cancellation stirred up a storm of worry within the Concorde project – if those guys cancelled, others would follow. The reason for TWA and Pan Am's decision was purely financial – the cost of acquiring the airplanes outweighed any possible profit from operating them. Even so, conspiracy rumours flourished, since the European Concorde project supposedly threatened American supremacy in the long-haul aircraft market. Neither the British nor the French government showed any signs of wavering in their financial engagement in the project – too much time and pride had been invested in it. Yet, as expected, other operators followed in cancelling their options for the plane. The Concorde was rejected by most of the world's large airline operators.

In January 1976, the Concorde started regular passenger traffic. The operators were now only two, British Airways and Air France, both government-owned airlines. BA served the London–Bahrain route and AF Paris–Rio de Janeiro. The Americans had been reluctant to let the plane traffic their country – Congress had voted for a ban on the Concorde the year before, but in February, the U.S. Secretary of Transportation approved two services a day to New York and one a day to Washington D.C. for a trial period of 16 months. The Port Authority of New York then banned the Concorde from landing the following month. In May 1976, both airlines began transatlantic services, but only to Washington D.C. It was not until November 1977 that services to New York could commence. During January 1979, ten service Concorde aircraft were re-registered for Braniff's subsonic service. The five British Airways aircraft carried dual British and American registrations, while the Air France ones carried only American registrations. There are photographs of a Braniff-painted Concorde, but they are fake (or possibly pictures of a plane that was painted on one side only), since the planes used by Braniff were ordinary BA and AF aircraft. The Braniff Concordes did have their own safety cards, however, with company logo and colours. In September of 1979, the French and British governments announced that no more Concordes were to be built, and that all unsold aircraft and engines were to be placed with Air France and British Airways. The costly supersonic adventure had come to an end. But the Concorde itself is alive. It still holds a tremendous attraction to travellers who want to experience flying at twice the speed of sound in complete luxury. Among the regular passengers on the transatlantic route are pop- and moviestars, businessmen and politicians who want to squeeze in a meeting on either side of the Atlantic, but still want to get back home for bedtime.

The accident at Paris's Charles de Gaulle airport on 25 July 2000 most likely marks the end of the road for the Concorde saga. In the first accident with a Concorde, 113 people lost their lives. Passenger flights did resume in November 2001, however, with the 12 remaining planes, five belonging to AF and seven to BA. Now, in the early 21st century, aircraft manufacturers are beginning to plan new supersonic projects. Thus, it might turn out that the Concorde, despite all its troubles, was 40 years ahead of its time. Whatever the case, it remains an impressive and beautiful aircraft.

Concorde

procédures de secours
emergency procedures

1-2. **Gardez votre calme,** éteignez votre cigarette. N'utilisez ni briquet ni allumette. Desserrez votre col, enlevez votre cravate, débarrassez-vous de vos lunettes, de vos chaussures à talons hauts et de tous objets pointus ou tranchants contenus dans vos poches.
Keep calm. Extinguish cigarettes. Do not use lighter or matches. Loosen neckwear, remove glasses, dentures, high heeled shoes, and any sharp objects from pockets.

3. Tirez votre gilet de sauvetage de son logement placé sous votre siège. Ce logement s'ouvre sur le devant.
Take life jacket from under seat by opening the front flap.

4. Passez la tête dans l'ouverture du gilet.
Place over head.

5. **Adultes :** attachez les sangles autour de votre taille. **Ne pas gonfler le gilet.**
Adults: Tie tapes around waist. **Do not inflate.**

6. **Enfants :** attachez les sangles autour du corps et par-dessus le gilet avec deux nœuds dans le dos. **Gonflez le gilet avant de quitter l'avion.**
Children: Tie tapes around body and over life jacket in a double knot at the back. **Inflate before leaving aircraft.**

7. Asseyez-vous et serrez étroitement votre ceinture de sécurité. **Repérez les sorties.**
Sit down and adjust seat belt firmly. **Note exits.**

8-9. Au commandement **"préparez-vous pour atterrir ou amerrir"**, posez le front sur vos bras croisés sur le haut du dossier devant vous. Appuyez les pieds par terre aussi fort que possible. S'il n'y a pas de dossier devant vous, croisez les bras sur les genoux et appuyez votre tête dessus.
On receiving the warning to "Brace", rest the forehead on folded arms against the top of the seat in front. Brace feet firmly on floor. If there is no seat in front, fold arms across knees and cradle head.

10. **Dès que vous serez hors de l'avion,** gonflez le gilet en tirant fermement sur le bouton rouge. En cas d'amerrissage, évacuez par les portes avant.
When clear of the aircraft inflate jacket by pulling firmly red knob. In case of ditching leave by the forward exits.

11. Le tube à gonflage bucal permet de regonfler le gilet si nécessaire. Vous disposez d'un sifflet pour attirer l'attention.
Inflate or top up using mouth piece. A whistle is provided for attracting attention.

12. Tirez sur un des masques et adaptez-le sur votre visage.
Grasp the nearest mask and adjust it on your face.

Concorde

consignes de sécurité
safety instructions

RENSEIGNEMENTS GENERAUX
Lisez attentivement les instructions suivantes, à appliquer en cas d'urgence :
— Rappelez-vous que le Commandant de bord détient une autorité absolue et que les membres de l'équipage savent exactement ce qu'il faut faire dans toutes circonstances et vous donneront les ordres précis à suivre.
— Restez calme et ne vous affolez pas. Quand l'avion sera complètement immobilisé, détachez vos ceintures de sécurité et soyez prêt à suivre les ordres de l'équipage pour évacuer l'avion.
— Les hommes doivent prêter assistance aux femmes et aux enfants.

— En cas d'amerrissage forcé, restez groupés dans l'eau. Ceci rend votre détection plus facile par les sauveteurs.
— Pendant la durée du vol le Commandant est en liaison radio constante avec d'autres avions et avec des stations au sol. Notre position est exactement connue à tout moment.

POSTES PORTATIFS
Les postes portatifs peuvent occasionner le brouillage des équipements de radiocommunication et de navigation de l'avion. Pour cette raison, l'utilisation de radios portatives, de magnétophones, etc., est formellement interdite.

GENERAL INFORMATION
Please, will you read attentively the following instructions to apply in an emergency situation:
— Remember that the Captain has absolute authority and the crew know what to do in any eventuality and will issue specific instructions accordingly.
— When the aircraft has stopped completely unfasten your seat belt and be ready to follow instructions of crews members for departure from the aircraft. Keep calm and do not rush.
— Men should assist women and children.
— In case of ditching, keep together in the water. This makes detection easier for rescue parties.

— Throughout the flight, the Captain is in constant radio communication with other aircraft and shore bases and our position is accurately known at all times.

PORTABLE RADIOS
The portable electronic equipments may cause interference with the radio-navigational installations in the aircraft. For this reason the use of portable radio receivers, tape recorders, etc., is not permitted.

TOBOGGANS ET CANOTS
Des toboggans sont disponibles à chacune des sorties de secours. Les toboggans des portes centrales sont également des canots de sauvetage.

ESCAPE SLIDES AND RAFTS
An escape slide is available at each of the emergency exit. The escape slides located at centre doors are also life rafts.

SORTIES DE SECOURS
Les sorties principales de secours sont les portes centrales droite et gauche et la porte arrière gauche de cabine. De plus, il y a une issue de secours dans la soute à bagages extrême arrière. Notez la position de celles-ci qui sont clairement indiquées par le mot « exit ». La porte d'embarquement extrême avant n'est pas une issue de secours.

EMERGENCY EXITS
The main line of emergency exit is through the R.H. and L.H. centre doors and rear cabin L.H. door. In addition there is an emergency exit in the extreme rear baggage hold. You are asked to note the positions of these which are clearly marked with the word « exit ». The extreme forward boarding door is not an emergency exit.

Concorde

SAFETY INSTRUCTIONS
CONSIGNES DE SÉCURITÉ · CONSIGNAS DE SEGURIDAD

TAKE-OFF AND LANDING
DECOLLAGE ET ATTERISSAGE

NO SMOKING

FASTEN SEAT BELT

OXYGEN

DON IMMEDIATELY
MASQUE EN POSITION

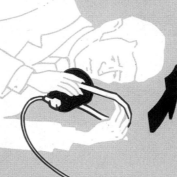

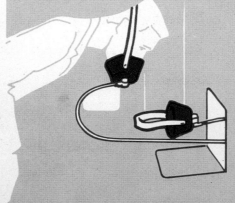

LIFEJACKET
GILET DE SAUVETAGE

WHIST
SIFFL

INFLATOR
(PULL LANYARD)
DISPOSITIF DE GONFLAGE
(CORDON À TIRER)

POSIT
E DE GONFLAGE
CHE)

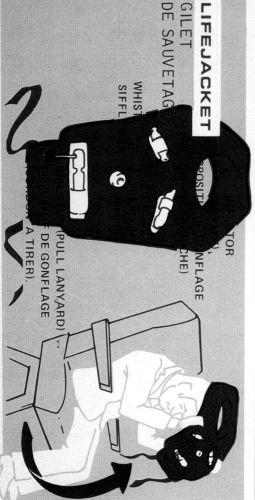

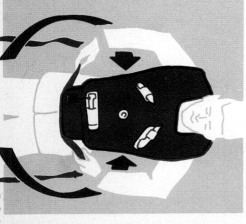

TO INFLATE
POUR GONFLER

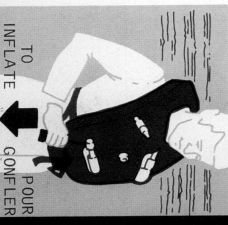

DO NOT INFLATE LIFEJACKET
UNTIL YOU HAVE LEFT THE AIRCRAFT

NE PAS GONFLER AVANT DE QUITTER L'AVION

Concorde EVACUATION

Issue 4   04/75

REMOVE
ENLEVER

BRACING
POSITION DE SECURITE

TURN HANDLE & PUSH/TOURNER & POUSSER

DOORS A

LIFT HANDLE & PUSH/LEVER & POUSSER

DOORS B

SLIDE
TOBOGGAN

RAFT
RADEAU

RAFT
RADEAU

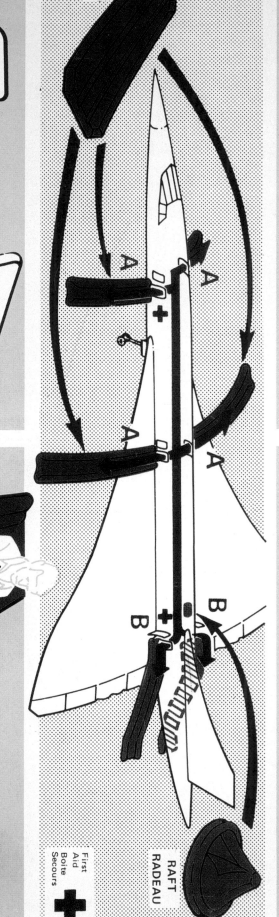

RAFT
RADEAU

First
Aid
Boite
Secours

✚

PRINTED BY TRANSART-INFLASTOR LIMITED, LONDON, ENGLAND.

Page 157 and page 159. Concorde "demonstrator" cards. These are two of several Concorde cards for use on customer demonstration flights and proving flights. They may look slightly similar, but the artwork is created for separate cards by British Airways and Air France, which typifies the entire project – the French way was not the British, and vice versa. Note the exit configuration, which was only used on the prototypes. The exit layout for production aircraft was different.

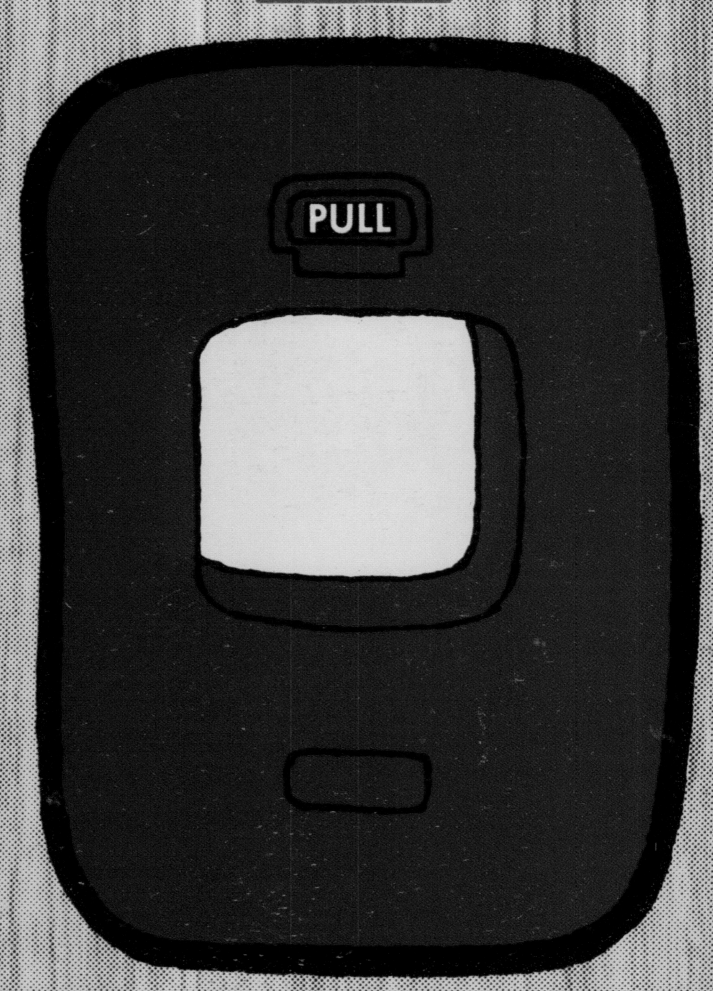

D ВХОДНА ВРАТА

Ex-communist safety cards

The instructions on safety cards from ex-communist countries are usually crudely crafted, and quite often wrong. Yet, this does not make these cards less fascinating. As symbols of cultural difference, the clash between Western technology and communist dictatorship, these cards are quite marvellous. Like all the other cards included in this book, they hold a mirror up to the time and culture in which they were produced. And some of them are beautiful, too.

Most of the aircraft from former communist countries in Europe are copies of Western planes. The most famous one is probably the Tupolev TU-144, a blatant replica of the Concorde supersonic jet. The Soviets were rumoured to have several spies stationed in and around the Concorde plants and testing facilities. The TU-144 was the first supersonic passenger aircraft to fly, and nicknamed "Concordski", it was a great triumph for the Soviets when the plane first took off in December 1968. But airline safety had not developed as fast in the Soviet Union as in the West. At the Paris Air Show in 1973, the TU-144 crashed, killing 14 people – all six on board the plane and eight on the ground. The crash is now believed to have been caused by a French Mirage fighter plane, on a mission to take pictures of the Concordski. The Mirage plane is believed to have disturbed the TU-144 pilot, making him pull up his plane too swiftly, and causing the aircraft to lose a wing and break apart. After the horrific crash, many doubted that the TU-144 would be anything more than a symbol of failed Iron Curtain technology. Aeroflot proved the doubters wrong when, in December 1975, a TU-144 departed from Moscow's Domodedovo airport for Alma Ata in Kazakhstan, 3,000 km (1,864 miles) away, but only carrying mail and freight. The route was discontinued after a couple of years. It was never an official passenger flight, although it often carried them. Consequently, there are no safety cards from the TU-144. NASA, the American space administration, acquired a TU-144 to carry out experiments some years ago, and still uses it today.

BALKAN IL 18

SAFETY INSTRUCTIONS

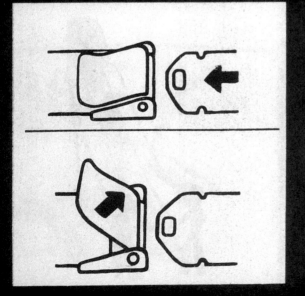

ПОЗА ПРИ EMERGENCY
АВАРИИНО LANDING
КАЦАНЕ POSITION

БАЛКАН ил 18

ИНСТРУКЦИЯ ЗА БЕЗОПАСТНОСТ

Моля, не изнасяйте инструкцията от самолета!

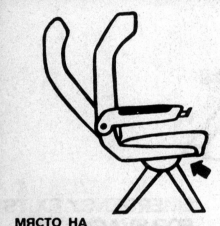

МЯСТО НА
СПАСИТЕЛНАТА   LIFE JACKETS
ЖИЛЕТКА   PLACES

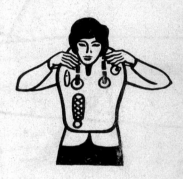

ОБЛИЧАНЕ НА   PULL
СПАСИТЕЛНА   THE LIFE
ЖИЛЕТКА   JACKET

ВРЪЗВАНЕ НА   PASS TAPES
СПАСИТЕЛНАТА   BACK WARDS,
ЖИЛЕТКА   CROSS AND
                 TIE IN FRONT

НАДУЙТЕ СЛЕД   INFLATE
НАПУСКАНЕ   OUTSIDE OF
НА САМОЛЕТА   THE AIRCRAFT

Please. do not take this card from the aircraft.

BEZPEČNOSTNÍ INSTRUKCE
ПРАВИЛА БЕЗОПАСНОСТИ
SAFETY INSTRUCTIONS
CONSIGNES DE SÉCURITÉ
SICHERHEITSINSTRUKTIONEN
CONSIGNAS DE SECURIDAD

IL 62

Sekyra
Топор
Axe
Hache
Beil
Hacha

Lékárnička
Аптечка
First aid kit
Armoire-pharmacie
Bordapotheke
Botiquín

Hasicí přístroj
Огнетушитель
Fire extinguisher
Extincteur d'incendie
Feuerlöschapparat
Matafuego

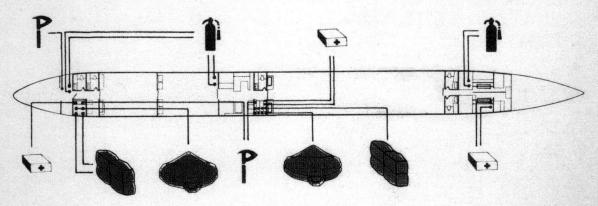

Balík s nouzovou výstrojí
Пакет с запасным оборудованием
Emergency kit
Baluchon avec équipment de sécours
Notausrüstungspaket
Paquete con equipo de emergencía

Záchranný člun
Спасательный плот
Life raft
Canot de sauvetage
Rettungsboot
Bote salvavidas

BĚHEM STARTU A PŘISTÁNÍ
В ТЕЧЕНИИ ВЗЛЕТА ИЛИ ПОСАДКИ
DURING TAKE-OFF AND LANDING

PENDANT DÉCOLLAGE ET ATTERISAGE
WÄHREND DES STARTES UND LANDUNG
DURANTE EL DESPEGUE Y ATTERIZAJE

Poloha opěradla
Положение спинки
Position of seat back
La position du dossier
Lage der Rückenlehne
Posición de respaldo

Připoutejte se
Надеть ремни
Fasten seat belts
Attachez vous
Schnallen Sie sich an
Asegurarse

Nekuřte
Не курить
No smoking
Défense de fumer
Nicht rauchen
No fumar

ČSA ČESKOSLOVENSKÉ AEROLINIE

IL 62

BEZPEČNOSTNÍ INSTRUKCE
ПРАВИЛА БЕЗОПАСНОСТИ
SAFETY INSTRUCTIONS
CONSIGNES DE SÉCURITÉ
SICHERHEITSINSTRUKTIONEN
CONSIGNAS DE SECURIDAD

Issued by CSA-TEI

Jak používat záchranné
plovací vesty
Как употреблять спаса-
тельный жилет

How to use your life-jacket

Comment utiliser votre gilet
de sauvetage

Gebrauch der Schwimmweste

Como usar el chaleco
salvavidas

Nafukování záchranné vesty stlačeným
vzduchem
Надувание спасательного жилета
сжатым воздухом
Blowing up the life-jacket by the
compressed air
Le gonflage du gilet de sauvetage par
air comprimé
Das Aufblasen der Schwimmweste mit
Druckluft
Inflazón del chaleco salvavidas con
aire comprimido

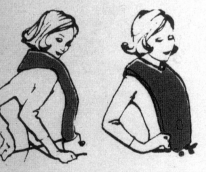

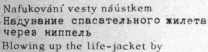

Nafukování vesty náústkem
Надувание спасательного жилета
через ниппель
Blowing up the life-jacket by
the mouthpiece
Le gonflage du gilet de sauvetage
à l'aide de la valve de gonflage

Das Aufblasen der Schwimmweste
durch das Mundstück
Inflazón del chaleco salvavidas
por médio de la boquilla de inflar

Plovací vesta je uložena pod Vaším sedadlem. Dá se navléci na tělo jako svetr.
Obě tkanice se ve výši pasu na zádech zkříží a svážou se vpředu na uzel tak, aby
neškrtily. Vesta se nafoukne prudkým trhnutím za šňůru u láhve se stlačeným vzduchem směrem dolů nebo náústkem, který je na vestě ve výši prsou. Nenafukujte
vestu, dokud Vám k tomu nedá člen posádky pokyn.

Спасательный жилет сложен под Вашим креслом. Надейте жилет так же,
как свитер. Обе тесьмы на уровне талии на спине перекрещиваются и
завязываются на узел спереди таким образом чтобы слишком не жмулы.
Жилет надувается двумя способами: резким рывком за тасьму у бутылки
со сжатым воздухом по направлению вниз, или же через ниппель, который
имеется на жилете на уровне груди. Не надувайте жилет, пока Вам не даст
указания член экипажа.

You will find a life-jacket under your seat. It can be put on in the same way as
a sweater. The two cords should be crossed at the back at waist level and tied
with a knot in front in such a way that they should not be too tight. To blow up
the life-jacket give a sharp downward tug to the string on the compressed air
bottle, or blow into the mouthpiece which you will find on the vest at the chest
height. Do not, however, inflate the life-jacket until instructed to do so by one
of the crew.

Le gilet de sauvetage est déposé sous votre siège. Il s'endosse comme une veste.
Croisez les deux sangles dans le dos à la hauteur de la taille et nouez les devant
en serrant convenablement. Conflez le gilet de sauvetage, soit avec l'air comprimé
contenu dans la bouteille en tirant fortement sur le cordonnet dans la direction
en bas, soit à l'aide de la valve de gonflage placée sur le gilet à la hauteur
de la poitrine. Ne gonflez pas votre gilet avant d'en avoir reçu l'ordre par
un membre de l'équipage.

Die Schwimmweste ist unter Ihrem Sitz aufbewahrt. Sie wird ähnlich wie ein Pull-
over angezogen. Beide Schnürbänder werden in Taillenhöhe am Rücken gekreuzt und
vorn so in Knoten gebunden, dass sie nicht zu sehr spannen. Das Aufblasen
der Schwimmweste erfolgt durch energisches Ziehen an der Schnur der Druckluft-
flasche in Richtung nach unten, oder durch Einblasen von Luft durch das Mundstück,
dass sich in Brusthöhe an der Weste befindet. Die Schwimmweste ist erst dann
aufzublasen, wenn ein Besatzungsmitglied dazu Afforderung gibt.

El chaleco salvavidas está alojado debajo de su asiento de Usted. Se puede poner
al cuerpo como un jersey. Ambos cordones se cruzan atrás en la espalda a la altura del cinturón y se hace con ellos adelante un nudo de tal manera que no hagan
daño apretando demasiado. Para inflar el chaleco hay que dar un rápido y fuerte
tirón al cordon de la botella que contiene aire comprimido, haciendo la maniobra
en dirrección hacia abajo, o bien se puede servir el pasajero de la boquilla de
gonflar con que está provisto el chaleco salvavidas a la altura del pecho. No inflar
el chaleco antes de haber recibido la correspondiente orden para ello por parte de
un miembro de la tripulación.

Děti mohou použít záchranné vesty pro dospělé.
Дети могут приемнит жилетов для взрослых.
For childern same life-jackets apply as for adults.
Les enfants peuvent utiliser les mêmes gilets
de sauvetage comme les adultes.
Für die Kinder benützt man dieselben
Schwimmwesten wie für Erwachsene.
Se usan los mismos chalecos salvavidas
por los niños como para los adultos.

LIFE VEST

1

2

3

4

5

MALÉV TU 154
Hungarian Airlines

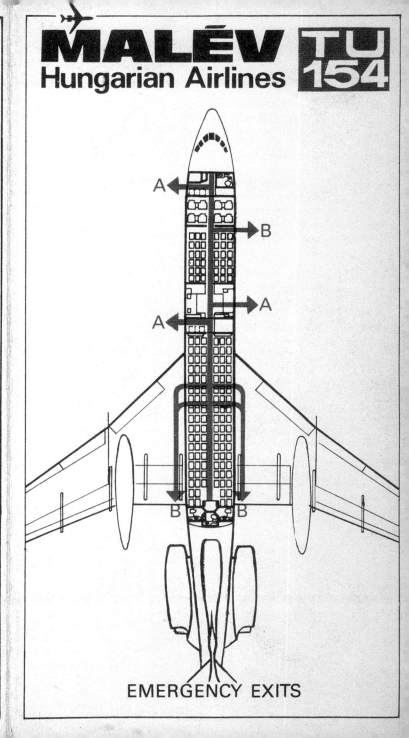

A
B
A
A
B B

EMERGENCY EXITS

FASTEN SEAT BELT

OXIGEN

1

2

ON REQUEST THEY WILL BE IMMEDIATELY PROVIDED BY THE CREW.
WHILE USING THE OXIGEN EQUIPMENT BREATH NORMALLY AND FOLLOW
THE HANDLING INSTRUCTIONS OF THE CREW

EMERGENCY LANDING POSITION

DOOR EXITS

OVERWIN EXITS

Page 167. Balkan, IL-18. Cards in this format were introduced in the mid-1980s and used until the decommissioning of the aircraft in the early 1990s.

Page 169. CSA, IL-62. This card is from the early 1970s.

Page 171. Malev, TU-154. This is the first Malev TU-154 card, from the early 1970s.

LAURENCE KING

Acknowledgements:
Thanks to the king of safety cards,
Carl Reese. Without your help this book
would never have existed. Also a big
thanks to Jo Lightfoot and Simon Cowell
at Laurence King Publishing, and thanks
to Henric Larsson at The Chimney Pot.

Sources:
Boeing
Lockhead
Airbus
British Aerospace
Cabin Safety
Lufthansa
Air France

For more information and internet links,
visit: www.designforimpact.com

This is a quality product from Der Kern.
For more information about Der Kern,
please visit our website:
www.derkern.com

Concept and design by
Eric Ericson and Johan Pihl
Text by Elias Modig
Consultant: Carl Reese

Published in 2002 by
Laurence King Publishing Ltd
71 Great Russell Street
London WC1B 3BP
Tel: +44 20 7430 8850
Fax: +44 20 7430 8880
e-mail: enquiries@laurenceking.co.uk
www.laurenceking.co.uk

Copyright © 2002 Der Kern

A catalogue record for this book is
available from the British Library.

ISBN 1 85669 292 2

Printed in China